Praise for *Finding Your Calm*

"Just when you think you know exactly how to relax and restore your energy, you realize there's so much more available to help you achieve calm! Discover the variety of ways these inspiring and knowledgeable authors are able to convey different methods to open your mind, body, and soul to heal and restore peace. The diverse approaches in this book are accessible and restorative and a gift we can all easily utilize!"

—Melanie Barnum, author of *The Book of Psychic Symbols*

"This exciting yet serene collection of practices, meditations, and helpful insights by authors, practitioners, and experts in their field delivers the chill. It offers a variety of practical suggestions, many that I never considered, to shake off the stress and burnout and relax and rest. In this busy, stressful, and fast-paced world we live in, this book is a powerful resource that you can draw from over and over for years to come."

—Sherrie Dillard, bestselling author of *I'm Still With You*

finding *your* CALM

About the Editor

Angela A. Wix (western Wisconsin) has acquired body-mind-spirit titles for Llewellyn Worldwide. She is a Certified Medical Reiki Master (CMRM), Certified Massage Therapist (CMT), ordained interfaith minister of spiritual healing, and intuitive medium-in-training. She is the author of *Llewellyn's Little Book of Unicorns* and has contributed her writing to *The Edge*, *Elephant Journal*, and *Llewellyn's Complete Book of Mindful Living*. For more, visit her on Facebook and Instagram @AngelaAWix. Visit her online at www.AngelaAnn.Wix.com/arts.

edited by
Angela A. Wix

finding
your
CALM

12
METHODS
TO
release anxiety, relieve stress
and restore peace

Llewellyn Publications | Woodbury, Minnesota

FIRST EDITION
First Printing, 2023

Book design by R. Brasington
Editing by Laura Kurtz
Interior illustrations:
    Llewellyn Art Department: 23, 104, 172
    Mary Ann Zapalac: 16
    The brain, in right profile with the glossopharyngeal and vagus nerves and,
    to the right, a view of the base of the brain. Photolithograph from 1940 after
    a 1543 woodcut. Wellcome Collection. Public Domain Mark: 133

Llewellyn Publications is a registered trademark of Llewellyn Worldwide Ltd.

Library of Congress Cataloging-in-Publication Data (Pending)
ISBN: 978-0-7387-7465-7

Llewellyn Publications
A Division of Llewellyn Worldwide Ltd.
2143 Wooddale Drive
Woodbury, MN 55125-2989
www.llewellyn.com

Printed in the United States of America

Other Books by Angela A. Wix

Llewellyn's Complete Book of Mindful Living (2016)

Llewellyn's Little Book of Unicorns (2019)

The Secret Psychic (2022)

CONTENTS

INTRODUCTION

Angela A. Wix

Do you feel anxious or stressed? Are you struggling with chronic pain or having trouble sleeping? Do you have looping negative thoughts and worries? Perhaps you're constantly in a time crunch, or you've recently realized your life seems to be perpetually fueled by adrenaline from an underlying sense of panic. Trauma, fried nerves, feeling wired, on edge, unsafe, overwhelmed, exhausted—this list could go on and on, but I'm sure by now you get the point. If any of this seems to be ringing a bell, you've come to the right place.

Just reading that list might have been enough to have triggered you into tightening your muscles, taking shallow breaths, and thinking fearful thoughts, so before we move on let's switch into a more positive mode. First, take a few deep breaths, all the way down to your belly, and feel your muscles loosen as you do. Picture something or someone that makes you incredibly happy. Maybe it's your pet, a friend, a child, or a partner. Picture their face and see them in a joyful state. Recall a particularly funny or joyful memory with them. Maybe it was your child doing a silly dance,

1

or your dog licking you in the ear because they knew it would get you laughing.

Feel better?

This simple practice is just one example of what awaits in these pages. Finding calmness is something that many of us struggle with. Thankfully, this book offers ways to tune in to your innate intuition, discover the right relaxation solutions for you, and lower your stress in-the-moment. It's unique in that it pulls from many types of healing, both scientific and spiritual, to offer easy-to-access and practical practices for issues such as anxiety and sleep. Whether you're already familiar with some of these techniques or are brand new to these types of alternative healing methods, if you're here with an aim for relaxation, this book is for you!

Soon you'll discover a variety of therapeutic systems and healing techniques in the form of guided meditations and simple calming practices, from authors with advanced experience in their respective fields who are deeply versed in mind-body-spirit modalities (if you'd like to learn more about any of the contributors, their bios can be found at the back of the book). You'll learn how to more effectively listen to your own energy and body and apply a wide selection of holistic options to support you where you're at. Best of all, this exploration offers a range of points of entry for what you may deal with throughout your life, making this a supportive resource for years to come.

You'll have the chance to explore physical, emotional, mental, energetic, and spiritual factors for finding a more natural state of calm. The healing space of homeostasis and energetic balance allows for optimal function in all systems. By understanding yourself and your needs better, you'll be able to make use of specific ways more easily and start applying self-care.

With twelve different methods, there's sure to be something here to help you find some peace and unwind a bit from the daily stresses of life. You'll learn about the language the body speaks, including physical pain that may be communicating stored emotional pain, and how you can listen to your body's wisdom to uncover what it needs. If your energy is constantly drained or you feel as though you're a very sensitive person, you'll understand what it means to be an empath and what you can do to support yourself, including practice in setting boundaries.

From the long historical practice of aromatherapy to the new odd (and fun) phenomenon of autonomous sensory meridian response (ASMR), there is so much to discover. Some of the most popular and widely available essential oils to help with things like anxiety, fear, stress, and depression are covered, along with blends and recipes for various products you can create yourself. While aromatherapy can feel very tangible in working with physical ingredients you can touch and smell, ASMR might feel much more abstract. This rather mysterious practice, sometimes known as "brain tingles," is something you'll learn how to access through visual and auditory sensory experiences to promote a sense of calm.

Gentle practices in visualization, meditation, chakra work, astrology, vagus nerve activation, and emotional freedom technique (EFT) can all make up powerful pieces of your self-care practice. Visualization techniques can be used to engage all your senses and bring peace to your life by encouraging the body and mind to relax and release tension that you don't want and focus on what it is you do want. Simple meditation can also be used to invoke calm at any given moment.

You'll learn about each of the chakras that make up your energy body from root to crown and how you can work with them to support your relaxation goals. In yet another form of personalized energy, you'll see how astrology can be used to help you find the self-care techniques that best fit you based on your sun sign. Ways to activate and soothe your vagus nerve when under stress is another fascinating option available to you. Creating calm through the vagus nerve can be considered a key to releasing acute and chronic stress. With the time-tested technique of EFT and tapping, you'll know what you can do quickly to change what happens in your energy body when you're triggered by emotions that cause stress, whether you're at work, before an important event, or as a daily practice.

When it comes to relaxation and recentering, sometimes coming back to the basics is essential. When we're amped up and stressed out, getting the vital foundation of good sleep can become a huge challenge. This is why we'll also address what you might do to improve the quality of your sleep, from integrating a calming ambience and reliable sleep routine to stretching, energy work, and connecting with spirit and your own intuitive messages in order to help you downshift from the day. We end with a focus on the importance of mindfulness as a way to promote gratitude and joy for wellness.

Becoming mindful, intentional, and set within the present moment has exponential rewards. Whether you're looking to relieve stress or anxiety, improve the quality of your nighttime sleep or daytime focus, ease pain and enhance healing, manifest new goals, or perfect your batting swing, entering a calmer state can be invaluable.

As you start to explore the various avenues for achieving an improved state of calm, make sure to keep a flexible focus. Instead of trying to speed through or create a new complex wellness protocol where you're trying to do everything at once, take it one step at a time. Whether you read through the table of contents and decide to jump to the topics that stand out most to you or start from the beginning and progress linearly, think of your exploration through these pages as a dip of your toe into the water. Instead of taking an intense dive into the deep end, immerse yourself gently into this relaxing hot tub of ideas and feel yourself unwind at a slower pace. Tab pages, highlight entries, or keep a journal to record the information and practices that are most meaningful to you. This way you'll be able to gradually develop your own personalized program that you can apply daily and fall back on when you're feeling most in need of tools to guide you back to your inner calm.

As someone who has always been wired for anxiety, I know what a challenge finding that place of calm can be. For many, or perhaps even for most of us, it takes daily assessment to check in and see where you're at for the day. Have things been extra stressful lately? Does the darkness of the season possibly have you swinging into heightened anxiety or depression that's leaving you feeling overwhelmed? Have you had a big change recently that's made it feel like life is out of balance?

Without a doubt, life is going to bring you stress. When anxiety takes hold or life feels like it's getting to be more than you can handle, remember there's a natural ability in you for relaxation. This is not to say that things like anxiety, panic attacks, and depression can be thought away or resolved through a round of visualization. Life and health can be incredibly complicated, and sometimes we need all the tools we can get! This book aims to provide you with a wide range of new ideas, perspectives, and practices available in your back pocket so you can be even more empowered in this challenging world. You carry a range of holistic tools that you can call on to remember the power you hold in bringing yourself the soothing, safe, secure sense of peace that we all deeply desire and deserve. May calm soon be yours.

CHAPTER 1

Tune In to Your Body's Wisdom

Emily A. Francis

Your body is chock-full of both magic and wisdom. Your ability to heal is so much more powerful than anyone has led you to believe. This is the beginning piece of the *who* within the body wisdom introduction. It's you! It has always been you! A beautiful masterpiece so delicate and yet so strong all at the same time. The body is a million different pieces all seamlessly fitting together to form a beautiful and exact puzzle that happens to be so exquisite that we could spend our whole lives studying the various aspects of ourselves and still never be able to get all the way through the webbing of information.

I would like to introduce you to your body through a different set of eyes. Eyes that have spent over twenty-five years studying anatomy, physiology, kinesiology, clinical and neuromuscular massage therapy, lymphatic drainage, craniosacral therapy, Reiki, yoga, taiji, and more. Not only have these eyes studied all of this, but they first had to learn how to heal from a debilitating level of major anxiety, panic, and agoraphobia. I had to find a level of healing that could help me create a new life; one that was filled with deeper body healing, awareness, and gratitude. I see the body through the eyes and hands that took over half of my life to cultivate. I want to take you through the who, what, where, how, and when of body awareness and its incredible ability to self-correct.

I believe that miracles are everywhere and opening ourselves to their presence draws them even closer to us. Our very presence is a miracle. Our bodies and all the incredible things it can do in any given second are a miracle. Not one single part of the body operates independently and that includes both sides of what caused any disruptions and what may bring you back into balance. At all times the body is working to maintain its natural level of homeostasis. Homeostasis is our body's regulating system of always trying to stay in balance. There are a million tiny little things happening all at once at all times of the day and night inside our bodies. Blood pumping, heart beating, nerve impulses, communication tracks all throughout the body. Through the nervous system (the brain and spinal cord), our body is receiving messages internally from everywhere and tries to respond accordingly. The brain is the motherboard of your body, always in constant communication and trying to do everything it can to keep your body optimized and working so well that you may not even notice when something gets disrupted. As with a computer system, and so with the body, there is always the possibility of glitches occurring. Some we notice and others we might miss at the time of inception.

We often compare our bodies to that of a car and with good reason. Cars can be quite sophisticated much like the body. For example, if any door is not closed all the way, a light will come on and a bell will sound alerting me to which door is open. It will let me know if it's the front side, the back side as well as if it's right or left. I check my dashboard to make sure that no check engine light is on, or that my tire pressure is low or that it's time to take it to the mechanic for a check-up. Our bodies communicate much the same way. Instead of a light on the dash, it's a pain in a particular area of the body that seems as if it came out of nowhere. It's a signal and a warning light. Especially if it persists and you can't trace it to any impact or injury. Some signals are easy to tell where they are coming from. If you ran into the table, you might see a bruise on your hip. If you were in an automobile accident, you will have pains and probably whiplash and you can trace the patterns of when it happened, how it occurred and find out what to do to get things back to their full range of motion.

But what about those little seemingly insignificant pains and signals that we wave off as random because we can't trace their original impact? Or what about on a deeper level that we suffer from something emotionally distressing but we don't realize it's been stuffed away for years just growing roots until it can no longer be ignored? Do we wave that off as a coincidence too? Pain is not random. It's never random. The body doesn't work in secret code. It works very straightforwardly in its distress signals. We just never got the owner's manual to know that when a certain light comes on from somewhere, it means something specific. We have to learn the language that our body speaks. And it is important to note that even as I offer you the areas that we tend to store emotional pain underneath a physical area (and I will take you through as much as I can in this chapter to help you develop your own communication with your body), what I offer here might not resonate exactly with the way that your body speaks. Everybody may have the same anatomical structures and the same constitution in most areas, but your body is only inhabited by you and that is what makes it incredibly unique. The way that your body will communicate with you develops with your awareness. You will feel certain warning signals differently than someone else might feel them. Trust that your body and your intuition once aligned will learn together how to communicate best for you and then learn to trust it. Trust your body above all else. What I offer here is a very detailed guide into our bodies in individual parts and pieces and then as a seamless whole the best way I know how. But I am not you, and you are not me, and your body will put its main doorbell ringer wherever you collectively decide to put it to alert you to issues arising. I mean this in the way that I will offer where we likely store our emotional pain and that is fairly universal, but the signal that your body will give you when that bell is sounding will be independent to you specifically and not on any chart I can offer here.

I may hear a song pop into my head and know that the lyrics are telling me something. This happens every time I work on someone. It's like a radio station in my head guiding me through while the songs change with different areas of the body. That is the way I can tune in to someone else's body. When it's my own body, it's a flutter in my solar plexus telling me to listen to my gut. I know the ways that my body is signaling to me whether it's about someone else or if it's specific to me. This took years of practicing and working as a team with my body. But it's not because I'm more intuitive than anyone else. It's simply a reflection of the work that I've put into making my body my ally. You can do this too. Learn the way that you best communicate with yourself and the world around you. Are you more sensitive visually, audibly, a deep knowing or deep feeling? Use this as your guide as you learn to allow these things to deepen your awareness of yourself and how you connect with the world around you.

In its natural state, your body is always working to remain in harmony. When something does get out of sync, your body is much quicker to send you a distress signal than you may realize. All the time our bodies are communicating with us and most of the time, we get lost in translation. What we may shrug off as a simple pain or ache is actually a signal that your body is trying to get your attention. When we don't listen at first to that original soft knock, the knock becomes louder and the pain becomes more intense. When we continue not to listen to the soft signals that our body sends us, it can turn into something far more destructive. By the time many people start to pay attention, the body may have gotten so far out of alignment that we have trouble tracing the patterns from which it came. This is when dis-ease among many other issues finally makes its presence known. This is also the time, in many cases, when people start to deepen their awareness and begin to listen to their bodies in ways they never did before. It does not require any sort of crisis for someone to learn to tap into the wisdom of their body and work in harmony in order to get back in balance.

Listening to the body is the most important thing I can offer in this chapter. We will first go wide with body knowledge and a basic introduction and then center in on what I know best: the muscles and how they relate to human emotion. I will offer what I believe to be four major aspects of the body. This is what I consider the *what* of the body. It's important that we understand the different and unique aspects of the body because the way that we approach each for healing is quite specific. Having this basic foundation is how we can create a tailor-made healing team specific to anything that needs support.

The physical body covers all of the physical systems within the human body: nervous, circulatory, digestive, endocrine, integumentary, skeletal, lymphatic, urinary, reproductive, muscular, and respiratory. All of these are physical aspects of the body. They all require the knowledge of a medical professional such as a general practitioner and a specialist according to what organ system to treat. All the treatments under this aspect are fairly straightforward with their handling in their healing and balancing. There are a wide variety of treatments out in the world for the physical body beyond conventional medicine, but in this aspect more than any other, it is very important to keep those medical professionals and specialists close. Holistic practitioners and integrative medicine are fabulous teammates in working with the physical body. Chiropractic therapies, naturopath doctors, physical therapies, physiotherapy and specific massage techniques all help treat the physical body.

The emotional body brings us into our thoughts and emotions and how they affect our general health. If there is an imbalance within the emotional body, it's not your general doctor that can help you find balance and healing. This is when we seek therapy: a psychiatrist (a doctor who evaluates mental and emotional disorders and can prescribe medicine), a psychologist (does not prescribe medicine and instead works with behaviors and thoughts to help someone process various grief, trauma, shame cycles), a psychotherapist (many times psychology in more of a group setting), cognitive behavioral therapy, hypnotherapy, EMDR therapy. This is a basic list, but I do offer highlighted treatments that have shown the most favorable responses. Treating the emotional aspect of our body is one of the most crucial aspects of healing if you believe that the state of the mind and the balance of the body go hand in hand, which I do.

The energy body often gets overlooked as its own complete aspect of the body, but it is very much its own person, if you will. I strongly believe this is where the magic keys to healing live. Also referred to as the subtle body, the energy layer of the body is a very important and particular piece of the pie. People whom you would see to help with your subtle body for healing go into the holistic therapies of acupuncture, acupressure, Ayurveda (though this and

Chinese Medicine encompass all aspects of body healing), yoga, taiji, intentional dance or movement practices, hands-on healing or therapeutic massage and energy work such as Reiki, therapeutic touch and/or healing touch, craniosacral therapy, pranic healing, sophrology, and much more fall under this category. Treating the subtle layer within the body can create powerful yet finite shifts within the system. I believe this is where big results occur where you least expect to find them. The energy body is tightly connected to intention and our openness toward healing. The subtle body the way I imagine it, is the place where the magnet can be activated to attract miracles.

The spiritual body is a vital layer in communing with our house of divinity within. This is an extremely personal and private practice in which I won't direct you more than the offering that this is the place where peace can be found within your soul internally along with the world around you. Practices may include prayer, meditation, centering, contemplation, studying spiritual scripts, etc. This is getting in alignment with the powers that be and understanding that there is something bigger out there than you all by yourself and working inside that flow however that resonates with you.

To get into these four body aspects more deeply, see my 2020 book *Whole Body Healing*. These four aspects of the human body require basic knowledge and a pathway of who's out there to help you find your way to deeper healing as you go. It is one of the most valuable resources someone can have. It is within our body and mind that we have the ability to shift and balance. However, it was never meant for you to have to face it alone. We can't learn everything there is to learn in this one lifetime about body healing. Therefore, we must team up with others out there who have dedicated their lives to the study of each individual layer.

I have had to gather various healing teams for myself, my children, and my clients to help people get their game plan together in order to achieve big-level healing. Things that may once have been thought of as insurmountable turned into success stories and miracle healing stories. Know that there are people out there who can help guide you and support your healing in big ways. We just have to know how to look for them and where to find them. This requires a level of discernment and a knowledge of what constitutes a well-trained professional in any given area.

The Emotional Muscle Body

This is the *where* of the emotions in our body. Where you carry your pain is not at all random. There is nothing that is ever random that goes on within our bodies, not on our skin and not within the deepest layers. When I was first in massage school, I learned that the psoas muscle is considered one of the most emotional muscles in the body. The psoas muscle is a deep hip flexor muscle located between the pubic bone and the hip bone. It also faces a high intensity set of nerve plexus' area of the spine. It is deeply charged and a vulnerable muscle to work with. This area tends to store emotional traumas of a more sexual nature due to its location and energetic attachment to the reproductive areas located closely. A person who might have had a lot of trauma with their menstruation (for example, fibroids, cysts, or sexual trauma) will very likely present in this muscle area. Many times, people will cry when we treat this muscle. It is a deeply freeing and healthy release when in a safe environment with a very well-trained therapist who can help you through it.

Learning this information immediately fascinated me, and I wanted to find more information like this. At the time, no book had ever been written about this subject, only passed down through the teachers in various massage and healing schools. This led me to a quest of over fifteen years of hypothesizing, testing, and studying what the other muscle groups in the body stored in terms of emotions. I began to recognize and follow a pattern of the places in a person's body that carried emotional weight and then could trace what emotions lived in which muscle group. As I started to question many practitioners beyond the massage community, I found that many things I had discovered had already been documented in a relatively close area of study garnering the same results. For instance, the glutes (the muscles of the buttocks) store aggravation and suppression. When we feel aggravated but don't say anything, we literally sit on it and into the muscles they go. In that same area are the Liver/Gallbladder meridian lines from Chinese Medicine. The Liver and Gallbladder govern the emotions also of aggravation and anger. I did not know this and yet I discovered the same information from working with the muscles and not the meridian channels.

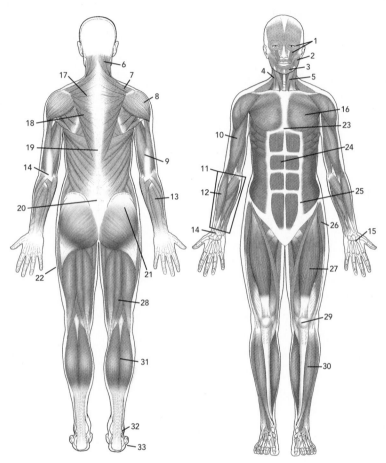

Emotional Muscle Body Chart

Head/Neck

1. Facial expressions: cheeks—smile/frown, eyes—true happiness or sadness
2. Jaws: tension and replaying of socially painful situations
3. Chin: muscles of sadness
4. Lateral neck muscles: flexibility and awareness of your surroundings

5. Anterior neck muscles: secret keepers of pain and trauma
6. Back of the neck: stress generally caused from outside influences

Shoulders

7. Tops of shoulders: weight of the world, too much stress, requiring excessive control
8. Side of shoulders/deltoids: also carrying excess baggage and embracing change

Arms

9. Triceps: pushing away, repel something
10. Biceps: embracing, acceptance

Forearms

11. Whole forearms relate to the throat chakra, speaking up and being heard
12. Extensors (tops of the forearms) repel, push away
13. Flexors (bottom palm side of the forearms) pull in, accept, bring to
14. Wrists and elbows: ability to redirect
15. Hands: the maps, same as feet. Helps assimilate information and feedback.

Chest

16. Brings in love or repels too much emotion. Correlates to the heart chakra.

Back

17. Upper back/trapezius same as tops of the shoulders: too much stress, need to be in control, weight of the world
18. Shoulder blades area: betrayal, being stabbed in the back
19. Middle center of the back: support muscles, strength in alignment with choices and movement
20. Lower back: fear of financial difficulties, fear of moving forward, loss

Glutes (buttocks)

21. Aggravation and suppression
22. IT band (begins in center of glutes but runs down the outside of the leg): confidence and safety make this muscle work well

Abdomen/Psoas

23. Diaphragm: confidence and trust
24. Abdominal wall: protection over vital organs and decisions within the body
25. Psoas: vulnerable, secret keeper

Legs

26. Hips: gatherers of information/decision making
27. Quads: protection, strength in movement, supports forward motion
28. Hamstrings: support muscles and offers follow through in movement and decisions
29. Knees: making decisions or feeling stuck. Forward motion keeps knees healthy.
30. Tibialis Anterior (shins): follow through on moving in a forward direction
31. Calves: Is your heart in it?
32. Ankles: the sweetness in life, are you allowing time for pleasure?
33. Feet: the maps. They feel, assimilate information and form decisions.

The body really is an extraordinary communicator, and it's important to understand that it does let you know what's really going on. To go over the body chart here with regard to muscle group and emotions stored, I offer an illustration taken from my 2017 book, *The Body Heals Itself.* Then I will discuss a few of the storage places that I feel are the most prominent among people. The tops of the shoulders hold the weight of the world. They hold stress, tension, and the place of overachieving perfectionism. Those who think that they have to do everything because that's the only way it'll be done right are where the muscles keep the pain of that behavior. Learning to delegate will be very helpful for people who keep tension in the upper shoulders and traps.

Next, moving down to the upper-middle back; this is where we keep betrayal. When we get stabbed in the back, whether this is something like a partner cheating on you, a divorce of your parents or yourself, or a friend betraying you, this is where you keep it. Even if it happened twenty years ago, unless you have done the processing work required to remove such an ache, it will remain behind the shoulder blades. Which side, the left or right, is important also. The right side is the giving side, so generally, this betrayal is something you may have had a hand in. The left side is the receiving side and so likely this is more of a child-with-parents-who-divorced situation. You had no control in the matter. If the emotions are not addressed in this particular area, you will likely be the one that continues to come for bodywork and complain of the pain in that area that you constantly keep. The muscles might feel better today, but inevitably, three days later the pain returns. This is when reiki, therapeutic touch, anything that can make you cry with full awareness that this is the area you are releasing from can offer healing of magnitude proportions. This will clear the chronic pain in that area when it's finally released with awareness and intention. A specific bodyworker who understands and can work in the emotional muscle body can help you release all of this from the very root. It's one of my favorite places to work with people. This area also sits directly across from the heart, so naturally, this is where you would keep your deepest heartbreaks. Working from the back side of the body versus the front side is also really important to help release stored trauma as the backside doesn't have the thick armor that the front side carries. It's like going through the back door into the heart area to help you let go of the old secrets and pains. Also having people lie facedown while working on the backside is always helpful too because they can cry in a more private way without anyone being able to see their face. The emotional release from the heart center is a deeply personal event and needs to be handled in the most considerate and gentle way possible.

Moving into the lower back area, this generally stores fears of financial security and of moving forward after a loss. The thing people don't understand is that the psoas muscle and the sacrum located in the low back go hand in hand. When one acts up, the other needs to be treated to offset the body. They work basically in tandem, both physically and emotionally. It is very important that your fragile and vulnerable areas be handled with knowledge and care. Or you can help yourself by stretching with intention and identifying the issues within those areas for yourself and talking your way through to the muscles as you stretch each area. Hugging your knees helps to release the low back. Rounding that area allows the muscles of the lower back to turn off, and that is what you want when you are addressing the pain patterns. The psoas stretch is somewhat basic but more difficult to explain in writing. The best psoas stretch can be done on the edge of the bed. Hug one knee into the chest and roll onto your back. The other leg needs to be bent at a 90-degree angle and try to lower the foot down below the plane of the 90-degree angle. This addresses the psoas muscle and allows it to stretch while the other side is turned off. Then do the same thing with the other leg. To me, these areas that I've described above the full back and the psoas are some of the most important muscles to be more conscious of. As you stretch with intention, create a mantra to repeat. Something like "you are safe and you can let go of anything that is not peaceful." When it comes to the chest and the heart space opposite the shoulder blades, a very easy stretch can be done to open up that area as you talk to it and help it to release any old pains that might be stored there. Simply walk to a doorway, place both hands on either side of the door frame and then walk forward until both arms are straight and stretched slightly behind you. Line your hands up with the middle of your chest and then look up. Give your heart a full opening experience while you work with the emotions that might let themselves be known now that it knows it has your full attention. Repeat something like "Only love may enter and all fear may exit."

Legs are about moving forward, and arms are about giving and receiving love and support. There is always more, but this offers the highlights. The neck deals mostly with awareness of what might be happening around you. There is a reason that the old saying "they are a pain in the neck" still lives on. How we interact with those around us is a very important piece of the puzzle.

The Somatic Emotions

In this section, I will introduce you to the emotions that the body keeps. "Somatic" means "body." This is the *how* of emotions are in our bodies. Beyond the emotional muscles, we also need to understand how to listen to the messages of our bodies. In psychology, there is a term called a "trauma capsule." This occurs when something is too overwhelming for our minds to deal with, and therefore we basically shove the trauma inside a capsule and then drop it and walk away from it. But where do you think that little trauma capsule landed? Right smack into the body. It plants itself like a seed into the soft tissues of the body, the muscles, the fascia, even the blood and plasma. We know muscles carry memory or we'd never be able to remember how to ride a bike or throw a ball. Muscle memory is scientifically proven. Now I'm simply deepening it. My work begins exactly there, with that capsule that fell into the body and ended up sprouting roots inside the tissues. I will give you a prime example of what I mean. Let's say a person is in a car accident. Instantly, because of the pain and overwhelm, the mind ejects itself out of the body and there is a disconnect instantly. This is a protective mechanism. It's too much to absorb and maintain a focus when something feels like an assault on your body. When I work on someone even on the day of an accident and ask them simple questions so I can get a game plan for treatment of their muscles, their memory of the accident will be very hazy. The mind ejects, but the body does not have an eject button. Every single moment of impact goes directly into the tissues of the body. The body memory locks it in, and it stays there frozen in time exactly the way it happened. When we are faced with a trauma, it's helpful to learn to listen to the story that your body keeps rather than only listening to your mind, which doesn't always report back accurately. How do we do this? Through an internal dialogue. I prefer to do this through visualizations and meditations.

What we want to do is find inside our bodies the rows of carrots that were planted when something impacted our bodies. I think of those plants as carrots. You only see the green tips on the top, but the carrot and the roots go very deep beneath the surface. Learning how to visualize going inside your own body to find the little lights around each carrot is a great way to learn to listen to the messages of your body. Once you find a carrot, you simply sit down next to it and let it tell its story. You can go to my website to go through every single body emotion of my somatic emotion chart through my audio meditations to pull them out while simultaneously filling the area up quickly with something safe. I also offer on my website free journal prompts to follow up with each meditation. Allowing your body to share with you whatever it's been holding on to is guaranteed to surprise you a little bit. Its story is not always the same version of the one you've retained all these years. The key to doing this work is that when you go back to listen to the story your body has kept, realize that you're only visiting as an observer. No need to be re-traumatized in any way. You know the story, you know the hard parts, but be willing to step back and simply listen to the parts your body has been needing you to hear. Then work with the carrots to remove them safely.

Somatic Emotion Chart

I believe there are four basic heavy emotions that the body holds: trauma, shame, guilt, and grief. Then there is an action bridge that either keeps you stuck or helps you break the ties that bind. Those actions are repress, process, and release. Once you have crossed the bridge past the release portion of the emotional journey, you will find four fabulous emotions. These lighter emotions are no less powerful and important than heavy emotions. They are happiness, joy, connectedness, and empowerment. For any given situation that still needs your attention, taking yourself through and over the bridge can liberate your entire body.

Permission to Heal

This is the *why* of body healing. Why do we want to heal and how does it work? As strange as it may sound, many times we get so used to whatever issue or setback we have in our lives, it feels almost naked and exposed when we find an option that allows us to finally live without it. Pain, fear, shame, guilt, and grief all become part of us, and a deeply woven part, into our webbing. When that gets removed, we may find ourselves pulling it back to us because we have no idea what to do in its place. That's why it is so important when we remove those carrots that have been planted within the tissues, that we quickly replace them with something equally as weighty so that we don't feel so empty without them. Filling those newly exposed spaces with a color and mental image of hot liquid that hardens instantly in the color and energy of something radiant and healing will make all the difference. We can't just remove the parts that have caused us pain without filling in those voids with something loving.

The most important part of working with your body to heal is giving yourself permission to do so. We are so conditioned to self-sabotage and guilt patterns that it can be very difficult to allow ourselves the happiness and freedom that comes with recovering any parts of ourselves that have been out of balance. This is the most vital part. This covers the *when*. The time is now. You must be willing to allow the healing to take place and stick. With every fiber of your being, you must agree to accept the goodness and radiance of your sacred self. My personal mantra that I play on repeat in my head during such times is "every cell in my body is correcting itself to function at healthy, optimal levels." You are a magical, incredible, and vibrant human being. You are not broken; you never were. You are whole and beautiful and powerful. Healing can be very possible for you, but you must get on the team that plays for the win. Everything needs to line up with your thoughts, feelings, and behaviors toward your highest joy and radiant health. You have to believe you deserve this because you absolutely do. Miracles happen every day all around the world; you deserve to have yours too.

CHAPTER 2

Calming Techniques for Empaths

Kristy Robinett

The eye of the storm is the center where the calm stays steady. All around the tranquility of the eye, destructive and chaotic energy surge but are never able to disturb the core center. An empath, a person highly attuned to the feelings and emotions of those around them, is often the eye of the storm for everyone around them. They are the calm and anchor for those they love. Even strangers see them as a safe space in their own personal storm of life. Yet, an empath often feels the exhaustion of the storm that continually billows around them. "I don't want to be an empath anymore" is a comment often expressed by an empath more than once in their lifetime. Carrying so many weighty emotions can cause an empath to lose their balance. Falling even slightly into the winds of the storm can push an empath hard into an emotionally unstable jet stream.

Am I an Empath?

You might have one or more of these qualities if you are an empath. There isn't a one-size-fits-all empath, which is why they are so special. Many empaths have at least two or more of these qualities.

You are a natural helper/healer.

- Complete strangers come up to you and divulge very personal pieces of their life.
- People often ask for your advice.
- You are a great listener.
- You often put others before your own needs.
- You might feel the physical and/or emotional symptoms of others around you.
- You tend to root for the underdog.
- Nature and/or animals give you a sense of happiness and joy.

Your mood shifts depending upon the energy of the environment.

- You instantly pick up on the vibes of the room.
- You struggle when you see or hear of anything negative or violent.
- Your emotions and the emotions of others around you have made you physically ill and/or exhausted.
- You are overwhelmed by crowds.
- You need to take time to recharge and restore your sense of peace.
- You are drawn to music or stark silence, depending upon your current mood.
- You get stressed around clutter.

- You feel the energy of the moon.
- Water creates a sense of serenity for your soul.

You have an uncanny intuitive ability.

- You are a natural lie detector.
- You trust your first impressions.
- You simply just know things.
- You have vivid and/or lucid dreams.
- You give purposefully to others.
- You are creative in either the arts and/or problem solving.
- You know who is trying to be manipulative but often get caught up in the drama anyway.

Types of Empaths

The following are some of the empath types. You may be one type, or you may have all these qualities. Whichever type you might be, they come with positives. The more you understand your gifts, the more you can work on them.

Physical: This empath will intuitively sense, feel, or absorb the physical ailments of another person.

Emotional: This empath will intuitively sense, feel, or absorb the emotional state of another person.

Intuitive/Dream: This empath is in tune with a knowing and higher awareness. They try to allow their intuition to lead the way.

Earth: This empath is in tune with their surroundings, nature, and the physical landscape. They feel a deep need to support the thing that is unable to defend itself.

Animal: This empath is deeply connected with animals.

Plant: This empath is in tune with plants, flowers, and trees.

Weather: Often called geosentient, this empath is connected to jet streams, weather patterns, solar flares, and moon phases.

An Emotional Sponge

I can remember back to elementary school when I felt the emotions of everyone. A teacher had a disagreement with her spouse the night before and I felt it. A classmate was depressed and I sensed it. The janitor was anxious about something going on in his life and I knew it. I walked past a parent and suddenly felt stressed by what I felt. My jaw clenched and my stomach hurt. I silently cried in the bathroom, even though I had no idea why I felt what I did. I was confused and frustrated so my release was tears, which was embarrassing. I felt alone, like a misfit, and confused. I carried what felt like a literal weight on my shoulders. It wasn't until years later when I discovered all the heaviness, stress, anxiety, and sadness I manifested as my own wasn't mine at all.

Like a sponge, I absorbed all the energy from everywhere and everyone. I walked around with an open heart and held on to everyone's emotional and energetic baggage. It drained me. I collected the broken pieces of everyone and made it my job to be the fixer, but I had zero understanding where to put the shards so they didn't cut me. Nobody asked me to do any of this, but I unfairly sacrificed myself as an emotional martyr and caused a mammoth amount of undue stress.

The Vibrations

Those who are empaths have a heightened sense of emotions they feel in a variety of ways. Some feel a vibration of emotion in their body. They might feel queasy, have mysterious aches and pains or chronic migraines. Some feel this vibration emotionally and sense something out of the perceived blue. Some empaths may be sad for reasons unknown to them. An empath might start crying, screaming, feel exhausted, or laugh for no reason. An empath feels all these emotions, and some shut down because it is so overwhelming. Empaths can fall prey to addictions as an unhealthy numbing mechanism.

Empaths have an extrasensory ability for feelings and emotions beyond their own. It can be a beautiful quality when understood and controlled. People feel safe and comfortable enough around an empath to confide their life story. Without taking the time to recharge or energetically balance themselves, an empath can consider this quality a negative and have compassion fatigue. This can cause an empath to feel emotionally and physically exhausted and sometimes stop caring all together.

You aren't delusional. You aren't broken. You are just used to giving away your personal power and claiming everyone else's emotional matters as your own. Giving away your personal power robs you of so much, including mental strength. Taking back your personal power and maintaining it requires you to make conscious choices. Before you can create positive change, recognize the ways in which you give your power away. It might be from complaining too much, spending time with toxic people, holding on to grudges, victim blaming, or fear of standing out in the crowd.

Why Am I an Empath?

Most empaths have at one time or another felt overwhelmed with their gift, sometimes referring to it as a curse. Understanding why you are an empath is important to finding balance and destressing to stay in the calm center of the storm. There are several explanations and reasons for why you might be an empath.

Traumatic Childhoods

Empaths who had difficult childhoods are often prone to anxiety, which can trickle down to digestive issues. They are often sensitive to the needs of others but may not feel that same care is reciprocated. Often what follows are feelings of being misunderstood and rejection. Past programming may lead them to feel guilty if they don't continue to people please.

Many who hear the word *trauma* think of the extreme kind of trauma, but the brain, heart, and soul don't distinguish the trauma of witnessing a fatality in a car accident from being yelled at for having forgotten homework in the front of the entire classroom. Your heart may hurt seeing a fictional character experience a breakup on the screen. You know it isn't real and just an actress playing a part, but it still might make you burst into tears. The same goes for different levels of trauma: it hurts no matter if it was small or large. Trauma is trauma, and an empath feels it on the deepest level.

You Were Born This Way

Sometimes you are simply born an empath. It might be inherited, or it might be because you witnessed those who raised you or your siblings emotionally going above and beyond and it became natural programming. It could be this is the light you were gifted within the world to carry not as a burden, but as a healer. You were chosen.

An empathic child's highly sensitive system can absorb more stress than others in all situations, and if there's nobody around who knows how to helpfully balance it, it can feel like a lot.

Family Dysfunctions

Every family has some dysfunction, right? The old joke is that it puts the "fun" in "family." An empath with family dysfunction is often labeled as the sensitive one and the peacemaker. Later in life, they realize that trying to keep the peace was a survival trait. It might've been a parent who inappropriately confided adult issues to the child. It might've been arguments in front of the empathic child or another type of conflict, sadness, or grief. The empath vacuumed up the darkness of emotion to balance the energy around everyone. Internalizing the struggle was lonely and triggers were created. Some examples of triggers are the phone ringing because they remember hearing that when their mother received the news of a death, or the sound of the screen door slamming because it was the last time they saw their brother. Or the sound of a beer can opening, and the empath knowing historically an hour later an altercation would ensue with their father. Other triggers might include smells, tastes, and anything else that conjures a negative memory. It also works with positive memories, but empaths seem to file the most sensitive and sad at the front.

The Lightworker

Every being is born with the opportunity to be a lightworker, whose mission is to make the world a better place. Not everyone accepts the soul goal or needs to have a purpose.

If you are an empath, you are also likely a lightworker whether you know it or not. Sometimes the lightworker shines their light so bright that everyone finds them in something like an open call for healing. However, this kind of openness leads to exhaustion. You are allowed to set the intention to how bright you shine and who you shine for.

Types of Lightworkers

Just as you can be more than one kind of empath, you might be more than one kind of lightworker.

> **The Activist:** You are courageous, go against the norm, speak up for what needs to be done and how it should happen, and stand for what is right.
>
> **The Inventor:** You love new ideas and come up with them often, see the world with childlike eyes, are determined, and see value in all points of view.
>
> **The Artist:** You see beauty in the simplest and most complex, are focused and eccentric, and like to see all sorts of viewpoints.
>
> **The Healer:** You have a passion to inspire others, are strong, often asked for advice, and incredibly intuitive.

Using your compass of energy and soul to create high vibration living helps create a center of calm as you continue to be an empath and/or lightworker. Being aware of the energies and emotions by consciously choosing healing energy and positivity can truly make the difference between feeling lifted up or feeling dragged by lift. It can begin with what you watch, what you eat, who your friends are, and even what clothing you wear.

Exercise
THE HEALING POWER OF TREES

Find a quiet space in nature with a tree that you are called to. Different trees have different energies, so you might want to seek out or think of specific trees to help your purpose. Pine offers wisdom and reminds you of your own inner knowing. Palm offers protection and refreshing calmness. Oak gives you courage and inner strength. Aspen represents renewal and new life. Maple helps you move on to new chapters of your life. Cedarwood helps you discover love and faith. Cypress offers healing with grief.

As you stand next the tree, see your feet planted like tree roots. Raise your hands high above your head and relax. Sway in the wind like a tree does in gentle wind. Do this for as long as your body, mind, and soul want. Then lower your arms and gaze upon the tree. Look at its beauty. See the ridges of the bark and any marks upon the tree. Notice how strong the tree is. Finally, give yourself a hug. If you feel comfortable, give the tree a big embrace. Take in any intuitive thoughts you might have. Thank the tree for its healing and wisdom.

You can also do this exercise in your mind's eye in lieu of going out into nature.

High Vibrational Relationships

An empath lives a lifetime thinking it is their responsibility to love and accept everyone, even those who mistreat and abuse them. Believing it will be different is harmful for everyone. You likely weren't their first victim, and you won't be their last.

Whether it's a love relationship, friendship, or family member, the following intentions/boundaries need to be established in order to keep things calm.

Listening instead of fixing: An empath needs someone in their life who won't simply try to fix them but will listen to their solid and crazy ideas.

Space and time alone: An empath needs time alone and someone who will trust them when they go offline and withdraw.

Honesty: An empath needs honesty because they often know and can feel the lies, which can be damaging in many ways.

Happiness: An empath needs someone who exudes joy. Realistically, not everyone will be that way all the time, but it needs to be more joy and less gloom.

Grounding: An empath needs someone who understands the need to be grounded and is grounded themselves or can remind them to be grounded when they start to feel heady.

The Negatives of Stress of an Empath

As much as there are so many positive thingss about being an empath—and there truly are—absorbing so much negative energy can be disastrous. These are some negatives:

- Being their own worst enemy
- Attracting the users of the world
- Being told and believing their feelings aren't important
- Thinking being sensitive is a curse
- Tendency to lose pieces of oneself while helping everyone else
- Forgetting that being happy is okay and it is up to them to make their happily-ever-after happen
- A loss of self-worth while holding everyone else up
- Feelings of guilt accompanying anger and sadness, including apologizing for how they feel
- Spending so much time absorbing everyone else's emotions that it manipulates them into thinking it's all theirs when most of it isn't

- Anxiety around certain conversation topics or people
- Strongly feeling a need to avoid certain people
- Receiving unsolicited commentary
- Attracting one-sided relationships
- Prone to loneliness and depression

Lugging the Heavy Baggage

Have you ever lugged a heavy piece of luggage around an airport? I typically take a carry-on and stuff as much as I can under the weight restriction. It is so exhausting. As luck would have it, the airline once forced me to check my luggage so I only had my small purse. It was the most freeing experience to walk through an airport without lugging all that weight behind me.

Metaphorically speaking, an empath lugs their own and everyone else's baggage everywhere. It might belong to those they love, those they don't, and those they don't even know. An empath claims it is their job to carry burdens, but it is not. Carry what you need and not what you feel obligated to carry. The good thing is that there are processes that can heal and free you.

Side Effects of Overload

An empath is often bombarded with requests to take care of everyone else, so feeling overwhelmed can sometimes simply sneak up on them. If you are feeling the following, you may be overwhelmed:

- Feeling drained, depleted, or low on energy
- Feeling frustrated, annoyed, or angry
- Having a lack of self-worth and low self-esteem
- Feeling blocked, stuck, or unable to move forward
- Feeling under-appreciated or unloved
- The need to cry all the time

- Unmotivated
- Attracting even more energy suckers or energetic vampires
- Feeling burdened by your natural gift of helping
- Failure to set boundaries and continuing to give and give and give

Recognizing Unhealthy Connections

There are several signs to look out for in relationships that are unhealthy. These are signs that it may be time to sever the cord:

- Feeling anxious or exhausted around a certain person
- Feeling stuck in life
- Obsessive thoughts about the other person
- Frequent physical illness
- Unhealthy habits to self-soothe the energetic drain

Exercise
CUTTING CORDS

Call upon Archangel Michael. He has a blue sword of light and helps sever negative energy that might be attached to your aura. The visualization doesn't take away the love or memories, but it helps clear unhealthy cords.

Light a candle or simply take three deep breaths and say:

Dear Archangel Michael, please surround me with your healing blue light. I give you permission to cut this cord between me and (insert name or situation), along with anything unhealthy you might see in my life. These cords do not serve my highest and greatest good, and I am ready for them to be removed.

Express your gratitude. Take another deep breath, drink a glass of water (think of it as a soul massage), and leave it to Archangel Michael.

You might cry or even sob. You might feel exhausted, relieved, or not feel anything. You might have to do the exercise several times for the cords to be fully severed.

Staying Calm in the Storm of Life

Everyone has had times in their life when they felt they couldn't possibly be handed any more stress but then were handed another stressful situation. You continue to do the best you can do and work on fumes.

Stress affects us all in different ways, and the outcome is normally not pretty. Sleep may sound like the simple solution, but the increased cortisol and the heightened adrenaline of fight-or-flight an empath often receives during a stressful ordeal may cause the opposite effect. As always, contact your physician if you have physical issues and see a mental health therapist if you are feeling burdened with depression and anxiety.

Exercise
PAINTING SOME PROTECTION

Envision a large egg shape around your physical body. In between your feet is an imaginary paint can with a paint brush. Take the brush and dip it into the paint can. What color is it? If you want to paint with intention, use blue for peace, pink for love, yellow for happiness, red for strength, orange for motivation, green for healing, purple for intuition, gold for understanding, and white or clear for all of the above.

Take the brush and paint the entire inside of the eggshell. You can even decorate it with glitter or confetti. This shell is your protection from vibrational beings who aren't aligned with your energy. Because you are a healer in your own right, they will receive the benefit of the color you painted your shell. You can even change the color throughout the day if you want.

Cracked and Invaluable

Kintsugi is the Japanese art of repairing pottery that lovingly uses gold or other precious metals along with lacquer to mend areas of breakage. It shows that being broken can be beautiful and scars can be healed and admired. The cracks are highlighted and add character, but they also add value to each piece.

Healing wounds, not covering them, is the best form of moving on. Below are several methods that can help you begin your journey:

Herbal cleanse: Burning herbs such as cedar, palo santo, basil, or lavender around your home helps remove excess energy that can cause you to feel exhausted, zapped, and overall stressed.

Florida water: Many spiritual workers use this, and it is believed to have cleansing and protective properties. It also attracts healing spirits. Sprinkle it around your home or wear it as a cologne.

Crystals: Many are said to have healing powers and allow negative energy to transmute into positive energy. Clear and rose quartz, amethyst, obsidian, and moonstone are a few.

Aromatherapy: Scents stimulate the smell receptors in the nose that send messages through the nervous system to the limbic system, which is the part of the brain that controls emotions.

Massage: This helps invigorate your body, mind, and spirit. If you can't afford it or don't have the time, put sea salt in the bathtub and gently scrub your feet. Reflexology is a wonderful way clear the toxins, whether from the body or soul.

Disconnect: Remove social media from your phone and unplug for a few days. You will be amazed at how much you will accomplish and how free you will feel when you aren't reading everyone else's problems and/or seeing others' lives playing out in front of you. Social media has become an addiction for many. Many people check their phone before they go to sleep and before they get out of bed. This invokes so many emotions, some good and some bad, but not always needed at certain times. Try to get a handle on how much time you spend with your electronic devices.

Spend time with family and friends in person: If you spend more time texting or messaging your loved one and they are in the next room, put down your electronic devices and spend more personal face-to-face time with them.

Hug: Reach out and hug a loved one or even yourself. Physical touch helps calm the brain.

Scream: Primal scream therapy is a thing. Get it out. Cry. Scream. Yell, but do it in a safe space where nobody is going to call 911.

Sigh: On the same level of screaming, sighing is a quieter option that offers a similar effect and offers a reset.

Laugh: I once took a laughing yoga class. You start off fake laughing, but over the length of the class, it becomes so ridiculous that you begin to genuinely laugh. You can also turn on a comedy or watch silly animal videos online.

Work it out: Exercise can help expel the icks. A walk around the block, a lap around the pool, or an hour of dancing can help shake the blahs.

Expectations: Miscommunication often messes up priorities. Nobody is a mind-reader. If you hoped for a romantic night and didn't get one, maybe you didn't communicate it properly and instead assumed your partner wanted the same. Have realistic expectations. These types of situations cause hurt feelings, sleepless nights, and stress.

Music: Music has a way to magically transfer energy. Upbeat music helps make you feel upbeat, while sad music does the opposite. Turn on the upbeat music.

Let's talk: Empaths often have a hard time talking about their own feelings. They instead want to help heal everyone else. It's important to learn how to express what you are feeling. It might be with a therapist, in prayer, or writing in a journal.

Healing work: An empath benefits from receiving healing themselves, which might be in the form of cranial sacral therapy, Reiki, acupuncture, singing bowls, or another holistic modality that aids in removing excess energy the empath is carrying.

Space: An empath needs consistent space to unwind and decompress. It might look like a walk, a drive, writing, or painting—whatever calls the soul.

Stillness: Solitude is the gift we give ourselves. It's a place where we can be inspired. Our soul is comforted, healed, and reconnected to our source when we pause and find the outer stillness to explore the inner stillness.

A Balanced Empath

Have you ever received a text message from someone you love, but you simply can't hear one more complaint, question, or need, and your immediate thought is *ugh*? You might let that text sit for an hour or even a day, but then you contact the person and abide by their requests, making you a dumping zone for what is going on in their life or requesting something from you. Then you continue to do the same thing over and over. If this is you, you need a crash course in how to set boundaries.

Without boundaries, you might feel resentful, burned out, anxious, and like a doormat. You know you need more sleep but wake up feeling sleep deprived. You might get angry at yourself and others for small things. You dread even the thought of certain interactions or people.

With boundaries, you will feel more energized, respected, and valued. You'll be consistent with self-healing exercises. You will discover or rediscover your self-worth. You'll attract healthier relationships and opportunities.

How to Set a Boundary

A common myth about creating boundaries is that you'll be hated and touted as controlling. Those who try to take advantage of your gifts may try to knock your vibration back down to their level so they can control you. Boundaries are not about control. They help you keep a healthy amount of self-respect. Here are some ways to practice setting a boundary.

Stay focused. Focusing on your emotions, thoughts, and triggers to certain people and situations will help you take responsibility for your own wants and needs. Focus on your needs.

Be specific. The boundary needs to be specific and something you can and will follow through on. Threats or ultimatums don't work. Boundaries set in the heat of the moment are not boundaries; they need to be specific and direct. Practice by writing it down. Repeating the boundaries according to different situations helps as well.

Be firm. Boundaries are a way of telling others who you are and how far they can go with you. Setting boundaries is about protecting yourself from undesirable circumstances that feed on your energy. Being firm and clear will set the intention that you aren't going to be wishy-washy and give in when and if the boundary is broken.

Don't apologize. Setting boundaries when you haven't done it before may start a fight. Explain that you have shifted and grown, and what worked then doesn't work now. Don't apologize for how you feel and what you need. An empath is often afraid of conflict and caves. Don't.

Logical and Specific Consequences

Being logical and specific with boundaries is needed, but logical and specific consequences are also needed. Here are some examples of what to say when a boundary is being crossed.

"Constructive criticism for feedback is helpful, but put-downs are not helpful. I will be happy to listen to you if it's positive guidance, but otherwise keep your thoughts to yourself."

"I cannot effectively communicate when you raise your voice at me. I will be ready to talk to you when you've worked through your anger and can speak in a kinder tone."

"When we go to dinner, I'd like to talk and catch up with you. I feel like I don't matter when you stare at your phone. From now on, we need to put our electronics away at the table."

"You have talked about my weight in the past and I've allowed it, but I feel very uncomfortable every time you bring up if I've gained or lost weight. If you mention it again, I won't continue to talk to you."

Practice and Revisit Your Boundaries

Unfortunately, you can't just set a boundary and be done with it. You must stay consistent. Even adults need to be reminded. Remember that your needs and mental health are valid. You can also alter your set boundaries according to your needs without an apology.

Exercise
HOW TO SET A BOUNDARY

Envision drawing an imaginary circle around yourself and name it MY BOUNDARY. Write down or make a mental note of all the things you will allow in the circle that are acceptable to you. These are people, situations, things, events, etc. that make you feel safe and are healthy for you. Write down or make a mental note of all the things you want to keep outside the circle. These are people, things, situations, events, etc. that are unacceptable in your world and are unsafe, unhealthy, or make you cringe. You may need to do this exercise several times a day until it becomes muscle memory.

Symptoms of Healing

As you continue to heal, you will experience a positive shift in your life. Acknowledge that your empathic traits are a gift and no longer feel so overwhelming. Take more time for self-care. Feel excited about the future. Realize you don't fear the things you once did. Don't be afraid to make big changes in your life. Take disappointments in stride. Sing along to the radio. Smile for no (or every) reason. Don't feel guilty about setting boundaries. Take your time. Feel energized and uplifted when helping others. You sleep better and wake up rested. Don't expect anything in return when assisting someone.

Once we learn to care for ourselves, we can better care for others. When you learn how to take care of your personal energy, you can better decipher what is yours and what might be another's. The biggest gift you can give to yourself is the gift of trusting your intuition, learning boundaries, and not taking on the responsibilities of everyone else. Learn that you can support people in meaningful ways without carrying their luggage so that eye of the storm turns into a calm you can keep steady in, whatever storm you face.

Recommended Reading

Aron, Elaine N. *The Highly Sensitive Person: How to Thrive When the World Overwhelms You.* New York: Broadway Books, 1997.

Orloff, Judith. *The Empath's Survival Guide: Life Strategies for Sensitive People.* Louisville, CO: Sounds True, 2018.

Robinett, Kristy. *Embrace Your Empathy: Make Sensitivity Your Strength.* Woodbury, MN: Llewellyn Worldwide, 2022.

"The Ultimate List of Spiritual Trees and the Magic They Possess." April 30, 2020. https://www.fengshuied.com/spiritual-trees

Walters, Kathy. *The Spiritual Meaning of Aromas, Colors, Flowers, and Trees.* Macon, GA: Good News Fellowship Ministries, 2013.

CHAPTER 3

Aromatherapy for Peace and Calm

Gail Bussi

"Calm" is such a beautiful word, evoking as it does a sense of peace and tranquility, of being at ease with one's own self as well as with the world around us, wherever and whatever our situation may be. We probably all know and envy people who seem to embody calm in their daily lives and effortlessly cope with any curveballs that come their way. Regrettably, I am not one of those people, and perhaps you are not either. Indeed, like so many of us, you are also finding it difficult to achieve or maintain calm in your life. After the past few years, there have been some fairly major shifts and challenges in the world that have left very few of us untouched. I would venture to suggest that there has been a sharp uptick in anxiety and panic disorders in recent times, leaving many of us searching for effective and gentle ways of coping and relieving these debilitating conditions.

Some stress and anxiety are normal and can even be healthy, in that it keeps us on our toes and aware of things that we need to work on and change. But excessive levels of these emotions are damaging both emotionally and physically, and they need to be addressed if we are to truly become our best, healthiest, and most joyful selves.

I am writing this chapter very much from personal experience, as I have suffered from generalized anxiety disorder/panic attacks since I was in my early twenties. At various times, I have taken mainstream drugs such as anxiolytics/tranquilizers to deal with these problems, and I have also had therapy and counseling. Let me be very clear: there is nothing wrong with these solutions. They may be vital at certain times of crisis, but as a trained herbalist and aromatherapist, I have chosen to follow the more gentle, natural path to achieving peace and calm for body, mind, and spirit, as I truly believe we do best when we attune to the natural forces around us and allow Mother Earth to heal and support us as only she can do.

The Magic of Fragrance

Aromatherapy is, as its name suggests, the use of fragrance to subtly heal, support, and uplift the human psyche and body; its use dates from ancient times, with both the ancient Greeks and Egyptians using it in rituals for protection, clarity of mind, and emotional wellbeing. Today this ancient form of natural therapy is more relevant than ever and is safe, effective, and generally accessible to us all. Fortunately, the growing popularity of natural healing methodologies means that most of us can find essential oils wherever we may live, and there is also an increasingly wide range of these oils available, including some that may be specific to our particular region or country. It's estimated that there are around 150 essential oils being used in aromatherapy today, but for the purposes of this chapter I am going to concentrate on some of the most widely available and popular oils used for relaxation and rejuvenation of mind and spirit.

Aromatic essential oils are, as their name suggests, the oil extracted from plants. All plants have such oils but they are found in different parts of a plant, such as leaves, roots, seeds, bark, resins, and, of course, blossoms and flowers. These oils, which are extracted by various methods—some traditional and others more modern and mechanical in nature—contain the very "essence" of a plant's healing and therapeutic properties, which is what makes essential oils the gift they are in so many wonderful and beautiful ways.

Just a note of caution: when starting out, it's important to discern the difference between pure, good quality oils and those adulterated with synthetic oils and other substances (these are often labeled as "perfume oils"); they may smell great for a brief time but contain few of the natural healing properties of the true oil. Price is often a factor. If oils seem remarkably cheap, that's a definite warning sign, similarly if an entire range of oils is marketed at the same low price. Genuine oils will vary in price depending on country of origin, the amount of plant material needed to produce the oil, and so on. Ideally you should go for organic essential and base oils, as these will have been produced in the most earth-friendly way, without toxic byproducts; such oils will be significantly higher in antioxidants and thus represent a far healthier choice for body and mind. Granted, these oils may not be the cheapest, but fortunately essential oils go a long way, as generally only a few drops are needed when making blends or other therapeutic mixtures; the oils also retain their properties/aroma well—often for a year or more, provided they are stored appropriately, in well-sealed glass bottles on a cool, dark shelf or in a cupboard.

Please also note that essential oils should never be ingested; neither should they be used on babies or very young children (up to the age of five) without consulting a doctor or trained aromatherapist. Similarly, if you are pregnant or breastfeeding, essential oils should be used with caution, and the following oils should be avoided entirely: basil and clary sage. Never apply essential oils directly to your pet due to ingestion or skin irritation. It's best to use the smoke/scent from incense, herbal wand, or a candle to waft around the animal instead.

How Does Aromatherapy Benefit Us?

Quite simply, our sense of smell is generally considered to be the most powerful of the five senses. We are said to be able to distinguish between more than ten thousand different aromas—some beautiful, some delicious, and some frankly revolting! This scentual ability is the one that is most closely linked to the brain, with an aroma traveling through the nose to the olfactory center at the base of the brain, where it is rapidly processed; in the case of essential oils their individual aroma and properties will be quickly received and disseminated by the brain. Aromatic molecules also travel through the nasal passages down to the lungs and then enter the bloodstream, further enhancing the therapeutic benefits of these scented oils.

If you have ever sniffed a bud of lavender leaf or rose and immediately felt a soothing sense of peace and calm, you've experienced aromatherapy at its simplest and most natural best. Research is being conducted in regard of the efficacy of essential oils for people suffering from cognitive diseases such as Alzheimer's disease, which will hopefully yield positive results.

Aromatherapy can be used in various ways for balancing, restoring, and healing the body on many levels, but here we are going to explore the particular powers of essential oils to create a positive, relaxed, and happy mental state. In turn, these states lead to a healthier body and a reduction in physical ailments that often accompany stress and anxiety, such as headaches, stomach pains, skin problems, and so on.

How do we calm and restore mind and spirit? Firstly, we need to relax, something often easier said than done. Holding tension in our minds creates tension in our bodies, particularly in the muscles, stomach, and skeletal structure. Essential oils work in various ways to bring about an easing of this tension, reducing or regulating certain levels of chemicals and hormones, such as adrenaline, in the brain. Lavender is probably one of the most well-known oils for relaxation, but there are many others too.

It's also important to create or improve a sense of wellbeing, being able to not just survive but also thrive in whatever situation we might find ourselves. Anxiety, fear, and depression lower our mood and make it hard for us to feel good or positive about ourselves and our lives; chamomile and bergamot oils contain compounds that work as gentle and natural antidepressants, lifting our mood and giving us the courage to keep moving forward.

When we are calm, we feel in balance both physically and emotionally; natural substances known as adaptogens help the body create and maintain this balance by either stimulating or calming as needed, and also by supporting the adrenal glands which often bear the brunt of exhaustion and stress. Essential oils that also work as adaptogens are (unsurprisingly!) lavender, rose, and geranium.

Sometimes stress and anxiety also lead to a lack of clarity and focus—something I know all too well! We worry about getting things done and spin our wheels mentally and emotionally but don't actually get anywhere or move forward. Some oils are specifically geared toward clearing the mind and enhancing concentration: these include rosemary, lemon, jasmine, and frankincense.

Favorite Aromatherapy Oils

This is a brief alphabetical list by common name of some of the most popular and generally available essential oils, together with a short summary of their properties / uses. Many of these oils are also my personal favorites.

Basil (*Ocimum basilicum*): Mostly considered to be a culinary herb, basil oil also has a long history of medicinal use, particularly in the Ayurvedic tradition of India. With a crisp and distinctive aroma, this oil is ideal for balancing and toning emotions and easing anxiety. It should always be used well diluted and is not suitable for use in bath oils.

Bergamot (*Citrus aurantium bergamia*): A favorite aromatherapy oil for many years, bergamot is fresh and fruity with a sweet aroma. It helps with feelings of fear, anxiety, and depression.

Chamomile (**German**) (*Matricaria recutita*): Best known for use in herbal tea, the lightly fragranced oil is also deeply relaxing and calming, especially when we are agitated or panicky.

Clary Sage (*Salvia sclarea*): Long prized in Europe for its medicinal qualities, this oil also calms the mood and lifts spirits, inducing a renewed sense of peace and possibility.

Frankincense (*Boswellia* spp.): This distinctive fragrance has been used since ancient times for rituals and celebrations. It's a very calming oil ideal for times of stress, exhaustion, and feeling overcome by fear.

Geranium (*Pelargonium graveolens*): There are many species of this plant, but this one, with its leaves that contain a sweet rose scent with spicy undertones, is generally the most popular for essential oils. It's suitable for adults and children and is a natural antidepressant and anxiolytic in times of sadness or great stress. I love it and would never be without it in my herbal apothecary.

Jasmine (*Jasminum officinale*): Probably one of the most instantly recognizable and beautiful fragrances, pure jasmine oil is expensive but well worth the cost. Its warm and uplifting scent is renowned for reducing stress and anxiety and creating a positive state of mind.

Lavender (English) (*Lavandula angustifolia*): This is considered to be the most popular of the essential oils, and with good reason. As a calming and restorative oil for the mind and spirit, it's second to none. Deeply relaxing, lavender not only reduces anxiety levels but also promotes restful sleep, one of the most critical things when we are anxious or overstressed.

Lemon Balm (*Melissa officinalis*): Minty and fresh, this oil is ideal for situations when panic and anxiety are making us feel overwhelmed and emotionally out of control; its mild sedative and soothing actions are helpful to induce greater calm and a sense of balance.

Lemon Verbena (*Aloysia triphylla*): The strong and distinctive lemon aroma of this oil has a bright and uplifting effect on the psyche, especially in cases of acute anxiety or panic. It also enhances focus and concentration, and helps us to feel more grounded.

Neroli (*Citrus x aurantium*): An oil from the blossoms of the bitter orange tree with a long and noble history, particularly notable for its ability to help with anxiety or depression. Its balancing and calming effects make it invaluable in acute cases of shock or stress.

Patchouli (*Pogostemon cablin*): A spicy and musky fragrance, long popular in the East and widely used in perfume blends, patchouli oil is also well known as an antidepressant that lifts and revitalizes low or anxious moods.

Rose (*Rosa* spp.): Nothing can really compare with the beautiful, fresh scent of the rose; rose essential oil is not only wonderful for beauty and magical applications, but also creates a sense of relaxation and well-being, particularly in times of stress or crisis. Rose oil blends wonderfully with other oils, in particular lavender, geranium, jasmine, and patchouli.

Sandalwood (*Santalum album*): Originally from India, this oil is derived from the sandalwood tree and has a sweet, woody aroma. It's used for anxiety and depressive conditions, as well as to promote restorative sleep. Because the sandalwood tree has become seriously endangered due to excessive farming, it's important to source oil that has been sustainably and responsibly grown.

Sweet Orange (*Citrus x sinensis*): The fresh, bright scent we are all familiar with! The oil, which comes from the rind of the fruit, will uplift sagging spirits, calm nervous tension, and help in cases of stress-related insomnia.

Thyme (*Thymus vulgaris ct linalool*): Widely used for both culinary and medicinal applications, thyme oil has a fresh, aromatic scent stimulating to both body and mind. It creates a mood of wellbeing when we are feeling anxious or miserable and refreshes the mind.

Vetiver (*Vetiveria zizanioides*): This is a deeply grounding oil for times of distress, panic, or grief. It helps balance the emotions and eases anxiety and feelings of being overwhelmed by a particular situation.

Base Oils for Blends

Although it is possible to use some essential oils undiluted on the skin (for example, lavender oil), in general it's best to use base or carrier oils as a medium for diluting and dispersing the oils; using base oils also allows you to create unique and personally therapeutic blends and helps make the essential oils go further. As some of the oils are quite expensive, this is a definite benefit!

I recommend all of the following oils, depending on your personal preference and budget. You can also combine base oils if preferred, using just a small quantity of the heavier oils, such as avocado, mixed with lighter oils like sweet almond.

Argan Oil: This traditional oil from a Moroccan tree is soothing, moisturising, and toning for the skin.

Avocado Oil: A softening and protective oil, naturally high in vitamins and minerals.

Coconut Oil: A soothing oil with a warm and nutty aroma; it tends to solidify in cooler temperatures and can also be greasier than some other oils.

Grapeseed Oil: Light and odourless, this is a mild and nourishing skin oil, high in antioxidants.

Jojoba Oil: Very similar to human skin, and suitable for use on all skin types, this is a richly moisturising and protective oil.

Olive Oil: Rich in vitamins and minerals, olive oil is generally an inexpensive and easily obtainable base oil that can be used for many aromatherapy applications. I don't use the heavier, extra virgin olive oil here—in fact, it's a good idea to use light olive oil, if you can find it.

Rosehip Oil: Particularly good in blends for using on skin that is irritated, dry, or mature.

Sunflower/Canola Oil: These oils are a cheaper and more accessible option, but unfortunately they often contain additives, so only use the organic varieties, if possible!

Sweet Almond Oil: A personal favorite of mine; it is gentle, soothing, and generally easy to obtain.

Creating Blends

You can make a basic fragrant oil by simply adding some of your chosen essential oil to a base oil, but creating your own fragrant blends of two or more oils is fun and allows you to make a blend that truly speaks to you on a deep level. As I have said, scent is a very individual thing, and it's often only by trial and error that we discover what really works for us.

In general, I don't like to blend more than three oils together but that is a matter of personal preference. Some people suggest using up to seven, though I personally find that adding more than three makes the fragrances muddled and they lose some of their individual charm and clarity. However, again, this is a matter of your own taste. If you like, start off with a few essential oils from the list above and experiment with fragrance combinations. You might find something absolutely fabulous that speaks to your soul and spirit, in which case I recommend writing down your "recipe" so that it can be re-created in the future.

Only ever use glass bowls, bottles, and droppers when working with oil blends; mix the blends in a small bowl or glass beaker starting with the base oil, then the essential oils, one at a time.

Pour the blend carefully into small, dark glass bottles that have a tight-fitting lid or cap (preferably with a dropper). Seal the bottles and then roll them between your palms to ensure the blend is well mixed. Label the bottles with the date and list of ingredients, and store in a cool, dark place. In general, it's best not to make large quantities of oil blends at a time but to instead use them up within a few months, to ensure maximum fragrance and efficacy.

Quantities for Blends

Here is a simple, basic formula for an aromatherapy oil; it can be increased if required. Please note that if you are going to be using the oil for elderly people, children, or those with ongoing health conditions, it's best to reduce the quantity of the essential oils by half. Similarly, if you are making oils for use in bath products, you can double the quantity of essential oils.

For every 2 tablespoons of base oil, you can use 10 to 15 drops of your chosen essential oils (6 drops for sensitive skin or other conditions, and up to 30 drops if you are using a larger quantity of base oil, up to ¼ cup / 65 ml—this quantity is ideal for making bath oil or salts). Please note that if you are using several different oils, the figures above represent the *total* number of drops used, not drops per oil.

How to Use Essential Oils/Blends for Calm

When we think of aromatherapy, many of us automatically think of a massage, which is a wonderful way of enjoying the fragrant benefits of aromatherapy along with the healing of therapeutic touch. Such a massage creates a feeling of relaxation, calm, and being pampered in a particularly magical way. However, we can also enjoy simpler and more accessible forms of massage at any time, for both ourselves and others.

Personally, I find a hand massage amazingly soothing and grounding; simply apply a few drops of your chosen essential oil or blend to the palms and the backs of your hands, then gently and slowly rub the oil in, using small circular movements with your fingers. This also works very well on the feet and is remarkably relaxing when we are feeling ungrounded or anxious. Oils or blends can also be massaged into the temples (great for tension headaches) or into the pulse point at the base of the throat. It's a lovely way to pamper yourself or someone else. My elderly mother, who was extremely anxious and stressed during the last years of her life, always became much calmer and more peaceful if I massaged her hands and feet with a few drops of a blend containing lavender, neroli, and geranium.

Other Ways of Creating Aromatherapy Calm

A bath, to my mind, is one of the loveliest and easiest ways of enjoying the magic of essential oils. Simply run a warm (not boiling hot) bath and add up to 8 drops of your chosen essential oil(s), or 2 tablespoons of an oil blend; swish around with your hand to ensure the oil is well distributed, then simply soak for as long as you like, inhaling the beautiful aromas. It's an ideal time to meditate or read a quietly uplifting book too. This is particularly nice before bedtime and will help ensure a peaceful and calm night's sleep. Please remember bath oils can make the tub slippery, so be careful when climbing in and out. You can also add essential oil blends to Epsom salt and sea salt to make relaxing and detoxifying bath salt mixtures. (Recipe ideas are given below.)

If you prefer taking showers, simply take a shower as usual and place 2 to 3 drops of your chosen oil blend onto a sponge or wash cloth. Rub lightly over your body, inhaling the aromas as you do so.

Room mists / diffusers / candles all offer a simple and delightful aromatherapy experience. To make a simple room mist, place 1 cup of mineral water in a spray bottle and add up to 10 drops of your chosen oil. Shake well to disperse the oil before use. To make the spray last a little longer, add up to ¼ cup vodka or 100-proof alcohol, and a teaspoon of sea salt.

Diffusers are specially designed for use with essential oils; the bowl section can be heated by either a candle or electricity and is generally made of china or ceramic. Place water in the bowl before adding the essential oil. As the water heats up, the fragrance of the oils will start to permeate the air.

There are many scented candles available these days, some more "authentic" than others as far as true fragrance is concerned. To make your own version of aromatherapy candles, you will need fairly deep pillar candles. Place them on a suitable surface and light the wick. After a while a small pool of wax will have formed around the base of the wick. Add a few drops of your chosen essential oil into the pool, taking care to avoid the naked flame.

It's also possible to create your own aromatherapeutic balms and other natural products; a basic recipe can be found further in this section.

Of course, the simplest way to enjoy the calming effects of aromatherapy is simply to add a few drops of your favorite oil / blend to a tissue or handkerchief, and keep it in your pocket or purse to sniff whenever needed. It's amazing how helpful and soothing this can be, especially in stressful situations.

Fragrant Recipes for a Tranquil Mind

As you explore the wonderful and calming world of essential oils, you will find your own preferred scents and blends: fragrance is an incredibly personal thing and very much a matter of individual intuition and choice. That said, what follows are a few simple-to-make recipes for soul-soothing products; they all contain essential oils and natural fragrances that help support calm, clarity, and peace. Note: All these blends may be mixed in 2 tablespoons of almond oil or other base oil of choice.

Soothing Oil Blends

Anti-anxiety blend: 4 drops each lavender and geranium, 2 drops neroli in 2 tablespoons base oil

Calming blend (for times of acute stress/panic): 6 drops rose oil and 4 drops geranium oil

Easing fear blend: 5 drops frankincense, 3 drops lavender, and 2 drops sandalwood

Greater clarity/mental strength: 4 drops rose, 3 drops basil, 2 drops clary sage

Grounding and uplifting blend: (a particular favorite of mine, very helpful when we feel out of touch with ourselves and the world around us) 4 drops rose and 3 drops each patchouli and frankincense

Peaceful sleep blend: 4 drops lavender, 3 drops each neroli and bergamot

Relaxation blend: 3 drops bergamot, 4 drops lavender, and 2 drops vetiver, mixed in 2 tablespoons almond oil (or other base oil of your choice)

Tranquillity blend: 6 drops jasmine oil, 3 drops frankincense, 2 drops chamomile

These blends can be mixed up and stored in small dark glass bottles and used in various ways: for massage, in bath oils and salts, and without the base oils in in diffusers and candles.

Other Calming Recipes

Sweet Calm Body Oil

Keep a little bottle of this oil by your side and use as needed. This oil combines sandalwood and geranium oils—both traditionally associated with calm, relaxation, and serenity—with a little bergamot oil, known for its ability to relieve stress and anxiety. I use sweet almond oil as the base oil, but you could also use jojoba or grapeseed oil. Add 1 tablespoon of the oil to warm bath water or rub it onto your pulse points and temples when needed. You can also use the oil in a diffuser or on a scented candle, as suggested above.

Combine the following in a small glass bowl: 2 tablespoons of your chosen carrier oil, 8 drops each sandalwood and ylang-ylang essential oils, and 5 drops bergamot oil. Mix well and store in a small dark glass bottle with a tight-fitting cap. Store away from heat and direct sunlight, and always shake the bottle well before using the oil.

Quiet Moment Pillow Mist

In addition to being a pillow mist that encourages restful sleep and banishes anxious thoughts and nightmares before bedtime, it's also ideal for use as a general body spray whenever you find yourself in stressful situations. Spray lightly over the body but avoid spraying it near your eyes.

Combine the following in a glass jug or bowl: 1 cup mineral or distilled water, ¼ cup rose water, 4 tablespoons vodka, 2 teaspoons aloe vera gel or juice (optional), 10 drops lavender essential oil, and

5 drops geranium oil. Shake well and pour into a suitable spray bottle or atomiser. Keep in a cool place and shake well again before use. (Makes about 1½ cups of spray.)

For another tranquil and relaxing blend for use not only in the bedroom but anywhere you feel the atmosphere could do with a pick-me-up, follow the recipe given above but omit the aloe vera gel or juice, and add 6 drops of jasmine oil, and 4 drops each of rose and frankincense oils.

When anxiety has made us feel sluggish and disconnected, this uplifting and refreshing scented mist is the ideal solution: again, follow the pillow mist recipe given above, but leave out the aloe vera and use 6 drops bergamot oil together with 3 drops each chamomile and lemon balm oil.

Soak Away Stress Tub Salts

Yes, I am using lavender again—for me it's the go-to herb for just about all applications and needs. Here, it is paired with the uplifting qualities of lemon balm, a happy and sunny herb and the sweetness of jasmine, another favorite. The Epsom salt and Himalayan salt relax body and mind, are purifying, and help to soothe and heal inflammation. Aromatherapy salts also make excellent foot baths for sore, aching, or tired feet.

In a large bowl, combine 1½ cups Epsom salt with 1 cup each fine pink Himalayan salt and coarse sea salt, and ½ cup baking soda. Mix well, then use a wooden skewer or chopstick to stir as you add 10 drops lavender essential oil and 5 drops each lemon balm and jasmine essential oils. Finally, add 2 tablespoons sweet almond oil and mix together well. This makes about 3 cups of tub salts; store in suitable glass jars, well sealed to keep out moisture. Add about ½ cup of salts to your warm tub, and swoosh around with your hands before climbing in! These salts should not be used if you have broken skin, and it's a good idea to rinse off well after your bath.

Tub salts can be made using different combinations of oils: you might like to try bergamot, rose, frankincense, neroli, sandalwood or patchouli.

Tranquility Balm

I carry a tiny pot of this balm with me at all times. It's like an aromatherapy treatment on the go! It also makes a wonderful gift for anyone going through a difficult time. The recipe can be enlarged as needed. In this one I go back to my favorite, lavender, and combine it with chamomile and neroli oils, both helpful in calming stress and anxiety, and promoting a peaceful outlook on life. Many people I know use these scented balms as a natural substitute for commercial perfumes.

Place a small glass bowl on top of a gently simmering pan of water (the bottom of the bowl should not touch the water). In the bowl, place ¼ cup sweet almond oil, 2 tablespoons coconut oil, and 1 tablespoon beeswax pellets. Very gently melt these together, stirring with a wooden stick or chopstick. When fully melted, remove the bowl from the pan and add the essential oils as follows: 10 drops lavender oil, 8 drops chamomile oil, and 6 drops neroli oil. Mix well, cool the mixture slightly, and then carefully pour into small jars or tins. (The mixture will thicken and should have a texture somewhat like soft butter.) Store the balm in a cool, dark place—too much heat will cause it to melt. Use within 4 to 6 months, otherwise the fragrance and therapeutic benefits will lessen.

Some alternative oil combinations to make different balms include the following:

For general anxiety and a low/depressed mood: 8 drops rose oil, 4 drops lemon balm, 3 drops frankincense

For fear (of whatever kind): 4 drops each sandalwood and neroli, 2 drops of basil

Traumatic situations: 4 drops each lavender and thyme linalool, 3 drops geranium

General stress leading to fear and anxiety: 5 drops rose, 3 drops jasmine, 2 drops lemon balm

In Conclusion

Hopefully you have found this to be a useful and accessible introduction to aromatherapy, particularly as it relates to the use of essential oils as natural healers and emotional support when we are experiencing times of stress, anxiety, and fear. When we are calm, relaxed, and at peace with ourselves and the world around us, we become most open to possibilities, choice, and change. Life no longer seems like an uncertain and frightening minefield but instead something to be embraced, a beautiful gift and opportunity, every day. Aromatherapy cannot, obviously, remove all of the problems we may be facing, but it can keep us gently focused as we move forward on a more gentle and hopeful path through life in all its beautiful imperfection and wonder.

May your journey be a peaceful and calm one every day.

CHAPTER 4

Visualize Your Way to Peace

Chanda Parkinson

Our minds have a tremendous capacity not only to store memories and information and employ critical thinking to solve problems, but also to imagine or invent the various scenarios or outcomes we want and desire for our own lives. One way this can be accomplished is through visualization techniques.

Visualization is the process where the mind focuses on a specific object, place, event, process, or outcome in order to imagine a particular desired result. When accompanied by guided imagery or guided meditation, visualization uses all our senses: vision, taste, sound, smell, and touch to build scenarios and circumstances the mind believes are happening in real time. The result is a powerful information loop throughout the body, cells, tissues, and organs, that responds by relaxing and releasing tension.

During visualization, our brains react in similar ways as if those things were happening in our real lives. When we visualize a peaceful place or positive scene, some parts of our brains actually think it's real. This can create a tremendous avenue of calm and drive us toward choices that allow us to feel successful.

Visualization meditation can transport you through your imagination to beautiful, serene, and peaceful places. It is the process through which we are led through a series of images, much like being inserted into the middle of a movie in our own mind where we get to choose the scene, the plot, the landscape, the characters, the scenery, the events, and the ending. It is the perfect tool for people who do not sit well in silence to meditate or who need something to help discipline their minds from wandering toward negative self-talk and other repetitive thought patterns that are depleting and anxiety producing.

When our mind is buzzing with thoughts, we can get stuck in patterns of thinking that are unhelpful and often trigger worry and stress. Disrupting those repetitive thought patterns is often like derailing a full-speed moving train. The culmination of this energy in the mind and body often produces an agitated state of being. The link between what the mind thinks and subsequently how the body responds has been scientifically proven.

Visualization techniques can stimulate changes in heart rate, blood pressure, and respiratory patterns, restoring a more balanced mind-body connection. As a practice, it can create peace of mind, a mental state of calmness or tranquility. A calm, relaxed, and contented mind promotes a balanced mental, physical, and emotional state. From that space of balance, we can better navigate our hectic lives and an ever-changing world. Ongoing visualization acts as a great stabilizer and one that over time builds emotional resiliency and stamina.

Visualization is like taking a mind holiday or a mind adventure. When we are given the opportunity to intentionally feed our mind images we wish to focus on, it becomes like a bedtime story for adults. There is a soothing, comforting space created that slows everything down. I highly encourage adding it to your nighttime routines to promote peaceful sleep and dreams.

The Benefits of a Visualization Routine

We live in an advanced technological age where instant information and connection to others is constantly available. The societal norm has become automatic accessibility to others through text and social media, which has created urgency around our social interactions and communication. Over time, the pace of modern living can wear on us and scatter our attention. Not to mention the readily available media sources that attempt to keep us adequately informed and help us navigate a world consistently in need of healing and change. No wonder we can't calm our minds or turn off our thoughts.

Visualization techniques disrupt the information loop, slowing our minds down so we can better ground ourselves in the present moment. In that space, we can be more responsive to intuitive impulses. Imagining an outcome through visualization connects us to our own creative potential and opens doors of possibility that perhaps we may not have even thought of.

Anyone can benefit from visualization. Top athletes are trained to visualize the outcome they desire before competing, not the outcome they fear or don't want to happen. It was realized over time that when the visualizations stayed positive, a positive outcome was more likely. You can use the power of visualization to change your own life, positively affect how you feel, manifest your goals, and sharpen your dreams. Visualizing outcomes you want increases confidence. It helps you practice success and grow to expect that things can actually go the way you want them to.

Here are just some of the benefits of visualization:

- Decreases stress
- Opens the mind
- Increases intuition
- Decreases pain
- Improves sleep
- Improves brain function
- Promotes healthy psychological functioning and well-being
- Strengthens focus
- Improves self-image
- Allows us to be more present in life
- Promotes feelings of gratitude
- Strengthens life outcomes we desire

Explore Different Visualization Techniques

You can listen to recordings and visualize through guided imagery, or you can completely make up your own visualizations. There is no right or wrong way to approach your visualization routine. However, it might be advantageous to experiment with different techniques, depending on what you are interested in manifesting. Some may work better for you than others.

For example, you may be dealing with a health crisis. You'll want to explore visualizations that help you create the outcome for your body that you want. Or perhaps you are beginning to believe that a career change is in order—you have some ideas but don't know what the next steps are. Visualization can assist you in daring to create the future path that inspires you. When your mind knows what it wants, your body will tell you through your own internal compass that you are on the right track.

Thankfully technology has provided a plethora of apps and other online programs you can use. Make lists. When you make lists of your goals, or journal your wishes and desires, you are activating the power of visualization. As you write words, and thoughts on paper, you become witness to them, and those images and scenarios can begin to train your mind and body to respond to impulses that are in alignment with those wishes and desires. Wish fulfillment is at first conceptual: you begin with a thought or idea and let your mind lead the way.

Obviously in the end, the exact outcome may not be the same as what you envisioned, but steering your own path in the right direction will harmonize your body, mind, and soul. To imagine an outcome through visualization connects us to our own creative potential. This opens doorways of possibility we may not have even thought of.

Visualization techniques we will be exploring in this chapter revolve around four themes: creating peaceful calm, healing our bodies, future outcomes for our dreams and goals, and spiritual connection.

Avoid judging yourself or analyzing how it's going during the visualization. Don't worry if your mind wanders. If you notice it's wandering, just shift by guiding your thoughts back to the scene you are creating. Begin by imagining the exact scene you want. Don't be vague or unclear. The more details you can imagine, and the more concentration you put into the scene, the better the visualization will work for you.

Tips for your visualization routine:

- Determine what you need to be successful
- Find a quiet, dimly lit spot

- Provide comfort features such as blankets, pillows, a yoga mat, bed, or couch
- Gather other mood enhancing ritual items such as soft music, crystals, incense, or candles
- Hike into nature
- Turn off phones and other devices
- Eliminate distractions
- Use an eye pillow or other eye covering

The best time to use visualization techniques is between moments of turmoil, change, struggle, or crisis. In general, visualization with guided imagery is not as effective when dealing with intense emotional responses brought about by grief, fear, anger, anxiety, or panic. Use it as a preventative form of self-care. Visualization is wonderful at relieving stress, though it does require a level of concentration and focus difficult to attain when dealing with chaotic aspects of turmoil or emotional breakdown.

Let's Practice

Stimulating all of the senses enhances any visualization routine. For example, if you are visualizing that you are at a beach, you want to bring everything you would experience there into sharp focus: imagine the warm sand between your toes, smell the fresh salty sea air, hear the seagulls flying overhead, and taste the cool breeze on your tongue.

A quick practice to warm up your own inner eye and imagination can include recalling a fond memory, perhaps a special occasion, something from the past that brought about joyful and contented feelings. Perhaps a favorite vacation spot or a day when you were immersed in nature.

You may choose to record the visualizations with your own voice and replay them, or you can read the steps here first and go through them by memory. You don't have to recall them exactly.

Visualization
The Apple Orchard
Practice Visualization

Since fall is my absolute favorite time of year, I love this particular practice visualization. Keep it simple in your own practice. In the beginning, choose something familiar and comforting.

Start by breathing in through your nose and out through your mouth.

Breathe in and out ... in and out ... several times as you begin to relax.

With each breath, your body begins to relax more and more, with the anticipation of a new inner journey.

Imagine, sense, and feel yourself walking in an apple orchard.

Feel the cool air on your skin. Notice where the sun is positioned in the sky, shining down its vibrant light on you.

Notice the landscape around you. How are the trees positioned? Notice if they scattered about or organized in rows.

Wander about getting a sense of the trees rustling in the breeze, and hear the sound of the ground as you walk.

Observe what is happening around you. Are you alone? Are there others around you?

As you walk down a row of apple trees, you see the apples glistening in the sun. See the colors, and imagine picking one to take a bite out of.

Unable to resist now, you stop and reach up, taking an apple off the tree. Take a bite and hear the crunch. Taste the juices and feel them running down your throat.

How do you feel? What do you notice happening around you? Give in to the delightful sensual experience of enjoying an apple in the serene surroundings.

Creating Peaceful Calm

The following visualization is for generating a peaceful calm state and to transport you to another place in your mind. You can use it as often as you wish to ease the mind by disrupting your thought processes. Use the Peaceful Calm visualization to calm anxiousness and relax. You can also use it when you would like to transport yourself someplace else that brings you joy and can support a gentle temporary escape from your current environment.

Begin by setting aside a few minutes so that you can relax without anything else you need to focus on. If you like, dim your lights, get comfortable, and turn on some background music to guide the process. Next, find a comfortable position. An easy way to begin is by focusing on your breath and slowing it down, breathing in through your nose, and out through your mouth.

Visualization
PEACEFUL CALM VISUALIZATION

Begin by closing your eyes and taking some nice deep breaths. Feel your body relaxing into a nice peaceful state of calm with each breath in and out.

Imagine a waterfall of healing, divine light washing down over your body, taking with it any tension, stress, aches, or pains. Breathe and feel the tension melting away from your body.

As the waterfall of light washes over you, feel your forehead, jaw, and shoulders relaxing, down over your torso and into your hips, legs, and feet, as you feel your whole body responding now to this beautiful stream of comfort and support.

Imagine you are in a boat, rocking gently back and forth on a river. It's such a beautiful day; the sun is gently beaming down on your skin, and the crisp air lulls you nearly to sleep.

Back and forth ... back and forth ... as you gradually travel down the river. You hear the birds overhead, see the clouds floating by. There isn't a care in the world right now. It's just you, the water, and the sky.

Continue to breathe slowly, gently, and comfortably. Take all the time you wish to enjoy the peaceful calm of the water, the boat, the birds, and the sky.

Let the rate of your breathing become gradually slower as your body relaxes.

The boat comes to a shoreline, and you slowly climb out now onto a sandy outcropping. This is your place of peaceful calm. It's where you can go anytime you need to escape, to travel away, to have a mind adventure.

Imagine what a place needs to be like for you to feel at peace. Don't leave anything out. This is your opportunity to have every detail exactly as you would like it to be.

Now create a picture in your mind of a place where you can completely relax. Start with the physical layout of the place you are imagining. Where is this peaceful place? It can be a place in nature, some place outdoors you long to be, even if you've never been there before.

Create an image of this place in your mind, and don't move on until you feel you have everything the way you want it to be. Perhaps it comes to you in flashes, feelings, or an inner knowing. Anyway it is created is perfectly fine.

Who is there with you? Imagine the people whom you enjoy spending time with joining you in this peaceful place. It's also okay to be alone.

Imagine even more detail about your surroundings. Focus now on the relaxing sounds around you in your peaceful place.

Now imagine any tastes and smells your place has to offer.

Imagine the sensations of touch, including the temperature. Imagine the details of this calming place in your mind.

Focus now on the sights of this peaceful place. Notice the colors around you, shapes, objects, elements, all of the beautiful things around that make this place a safe haven of comfort and support.

What are you doing in this calming place? Perhaps you are just sitting, listening to the sounds, and observing the happenings in your surroundings.

Maybe you find yourself magically floating about the space, exploring what else there is to discover.

This is a place where you have no worries, cares, or concerns. It's a place where you can simply rejuvenate, relax, and enjoy just being.

Continue to enjoy your peaceful place. If you should be uncomfortable at any point, move or shift your body and make any necessary adjustments to become more comfortable.

Memorize the sights, sounds, and sensations around you. This is the place you can come back to often as a mini-getaway from the pressures or burdens of regular life and responsibilities.

After you have thoroughly visualized this place and are ready to leave, allow yourself to come back into the room and leave your safe place for now, knowing that you can return to your safe place at any time you like.

Feel yourself returning to the present space. Notice your surroundings, move your fingers and toes, and begin to open your eyes, alert and returned.

Allow this feeling of peace and calm to follow you throughout the rest of your day. Your safe place is available to you whenever you need to go there.

Healing Our Bodies

The following visualization facilitates healing throughout our physical bodies as our mind guides the process. Using your mind to talk to your own body, directing its healing release, is a readily available tool.

With so many competing priorities, not to mention the state of the world as it seeks to stabilize in the wake of a pandemic, there is a cost to our mental health that simply living in society during this time can trigger. We are all dealing with upheaval and war in other countries, seeking to rectify massive social justice and human rights violations, and the dire effects of climate change. As we seek to navigate this new world, it can be constantly coming at us. We are inevitably experiencing our own exhaustion and supporting others as they work to orient themselves in our world. This leads to something known as empathy fatigue. We can drain our empathy account, leaving us with some pretty dark emotional states.

We are not only dealing with our own responses to what is happening around us but also supporting and loving those who are suffering and in pain. It is easy to absorb the energy and emotions of others if we aren't careful, and this can negatively affect our frame of mind and moods. Use the following visualization to combat the buildup of energy in the form of thoughts, feelings, or emotions that don't belong to you.

Empathy fatigue symptoms can include:

- Feeling tense or agitated
- Not feeling like being around others
- Feeling numb and disconnected
- Lacking energy to accomplish basic things
- Obsessive thoughts about the suffering of others
- Shame, guilt, and self-blame
- Feelings of rage, anger, and sadness

The Self-Healing visualization takes it one step further. Not only does it address the emotional implications of stress and empathy fatigue, it also directly addresses areas in our bodies where we have previously mishandled energy, have become burned out from unresolved issues, or inadvertently stored up energy that isn't ours. This visualization is one way to safely release it all.

It's an effective and simple method to scan the body and focus on releasing, recycling energy and bringing it back up as healing light. During illness, visualize the healing hand of the divine or gifted spiritual masters coming to lay hands on your body, to assist, manipulate, and move the illness or diseased parts of your own body.

Physical symptoms can include:

- Constant feelings of deep exhaustion
- Nausea and digestion issues

- Self-medicating with food, drugs, or alcohol
- Relationship issues
- Avoiding important responsibilities
- Insomnia
- Racing thoughts

Visualization
SELF-HEALING VISUALIZATION

Begin by finding a comfortable, relaxed position. Allow your body to begin to relax. Close your eyes.

Breathe in … and out … creating a steady rhythm of breath now, begin to feel your body succumb to the rich waves of relaxation your breath induces.

As you continue to breathe, imagine the entire room you are in filling with bright white light. This light comes from a divine place filled with love and infused with healing energy.

Take a cleansing breath in now, and when you breathe in, pull that bright light into your body. Breathe out the tension, aches, or discomfort in your body.

As you breathe in, more of that divine healing light comes into your body, and you can see or sense it traveling throughout your body now going to where it's needed.

Feel it surging toward the bottoms of your feet. It might feel like stepping into a warm bathtub … or it may feel like a tingling sensation … or simply calm and loose. Allow this healing to spread over your feet and up to your ankles.

Feel this healing energy now rising above your ankles, flowing up your lower legs to your knees, continuing up to your upper legs to your thighs.

Breathe in and out … and as you remove healing light from the room, more floods the space, an endless stream of continuous light. It continues to spread throughout your body, rising up now to your hips … to your stomach and lower back.

Feel your physical body responding now, the organs in your abdomen and mid-section feeling a warmth, a revitalization; allow that energy to drive deeper into your cells and tissues, muscles and bones.

Now it rises up to your torso and upper back, then travels through your shoulders to your collarbone … then down your arms into your wrists, hands, fingers, and joints.

Feel this healing pulse of energy race toward the palms of your hands, which are powerful healing centers in your own body.

Bring the healing energy now to your chin and jaw, around to the back of your neck, cheeks, nose, eyes. Feel your eyelids growing heavier and more relaxed now, responding to the bliss of this magnificent healing energy.

The healing light now courses through your spine, up and down … up and down … impacting the nervous system, making the nerve endings respond with joy. It spreads out from there deeply into your lungs and heart, through the organs in your torso and chest. You begin to feel energized now.

Continue to breathe smoothly and slowly as you mentally scan your body, sending any further healing to areas of concern. Allow that healing to concentrate its energy even brighter in those spaces that need it the most.

Imagine that the air you are breathing can cleanse your body and remove any toxicity or impurities, and begin to repair any damage. Imagine that each breath in carries healing.

Finally, see, sense, and feel your own body as complete and whole. You have moved a lot of stagnant energy. See and sense that stagnant energy, a dark shadow leaving your body, dissipating into the sky, transformed into beautiful butterflies floating away, never to return.

Breathe a few more cleansing breaths and come back, then open your eyes. Slowly get up and get a nice glass of clean water. If you feel like moving your body, you can do gentle stretching, or take a walk. Other appropriate activities: a nice warm bath with essential oils, a nap, sit in the sun with a pet or read a book. Be gentle knowing you have positively impacted your physical body and begun to infuse healing energies.

Visualizing Future Outcomes for Our Goals and Dreams

Many of the world's successful musicians, artists, athletes, entrepreneurs, and authors use visualization techniques. It helps them maintain disciplined focus toward a desired outcome. When Oprah Winfrey wanted the role she played in *The Color Purple*, she envisioned being in the movie nonstop for months. When it finally came to fruition, she fully credited her nonstop positive thinking and visualizing that outcome, knowing she was the right person for that role all along. Michael Phelps, Olympic swimmer, also uses visualization. You have the opportunity to join the throngs of successful people in our world by altering your brain waves and thought patterns.

Choosing one goal at a time to visualize makes the process more focused and specific to something you actually want to achieve verses waiting for it to come to you. Picture the scene exactly as you imagine it unfolding. Decide what you are wearing, what color the walls are in the room, hear the rustling of papers on a table, smell the fresh coffee brewing, see the smiling faces of others around you, feel the collaborative energies.

There are certain important things to consider before engaging in visualization for goal achievement. First, stay focused on what you want, not what you don't want. It's easy to slip into a loop of doubtful thinking, and this can easily derail the train you're on. Disrupt intrusive thoughts by bringing your mind back to the outcome you want. Next, believe that you will have what you want and take action toward your goal. This keeps the energy moving you toward it, and continues to align you with your goal. Finally, let go of having to control the exact process of getting there. Sometimes it's exactly as you see it, and other times it's a variation on your vision. How to get there isn't as important as keeping your mind and heart focused on the target. The details often work themselves out for you.

More tips for visualizing future outcomes: write down words, a mantra, or a sentence that describes the outcome you want. Put it on your bathroom mirror, your car dash, inside a closet door, or some other place you see every day. Find an image or object that represents your goal or what you are seeking to accomplish. Put that object or image someplace you will see often, such as in a handbag or on your desk at home or at work.

Take it a step further by creating a vision board for your goals and dreams. A vision board is a physical representation in images of what you want. Cut out pictures from magazines, or print out pictures from the internet and paste them together in a collage of images. The images should be authentic to you and achievable through focused action. Place your vision board somewhere you see often. Watch the magic unfold.

Visualization
GOAL ACHIEVEMENT VISUALIZATION

A comfortable seated position is sufficient for this particular visualization. You may also choose to recline, or lie on the floor or a bed—whatever will allow you to remain awake and engaged in the process.

You can have your palms facing up and open to promote feelings of openness. Or if you prefer, you can lie on your stomach to safely explore and feel grounded at the same time.

Keep your eyes open and fixed on a spot directly across the room, or on the ceiling if you are lying down. If you can stay awake, you may choose to close your eyes.

Inhale through your nose and exhale through your mouth, releasing tension. With each breath, feel yourself coming fully into your body, present, and ready to focus on your goals and future path.

Take another series of inhales and exhales, each one bringing you deeper into a state of relaxation, feeling the outside world disappearing with each breath.

It feels so good just to be here. Continue with intentional breaths for as long as you wish before moving on.

Know that now, in this moment, you can unwind and relax, knowing that everything that is meant for you is already on its way to you.

Continue to anchor yourself in present awareness through your softening breaths. On your exhale, release any pressure inside, that has been building up throughout your day, perhaps your week.

Let your shoulders surrender to gravity, breathing normally now; there is no effort at this moment.

Now shift your awareness inward, and visualize yourself at the very moment when you have achieved an important goal, dream, or wish. At this moment, you are in your body experiencing exactly what your goal is.

How do you feel at this moment?

Where are you? Use your senses fully to see, hear, and feel everything around you, as if it is happening. What is the temperature like on your skin?

I invite you to take a few minutes to explore this moment of goal fulfillment and everything you imagine or dream that it entails.

What are your emotions right now? How about your facial expression?

You have achieved your goal. You have completely realized your intentions. Allow the magic of this moment to permeate the core of your being.

Notice if there is anything running through your mind. An edge of doubt or fear? Be gentle with that doubt or fear, and invite it to step aside; it's not welcome now.

See, sense, or feel your future self opening a notebook and a pen, and writing down all of the things you are grateful for. Who helped you get to your goal? What worked to get you to this point?

When you are ready, slowly close the notebook, and remain in the good vibe of these emotions for as long as you wish. Remaining with the good emotions of this accomplishment locks in a piece of your own courage, strength, and determination to persevere when things get rough.

Gently come back to the room, take a few more deep breaths and ground yourself in your body, and perhaps spend time writing about what you experienced.

What are *three* action steps you can take immediately toward your goal?

Spiritual Connection

As a spirit occupying a human physical body, it can be easy to get lost in our own lives, our egos eagerly running the show. Our modern busy lives can keep us substantially disconnected from our own inner essence, that pure light of our core, which is where we experience true freedom and release. Our inner light thrives when it is given acknowledgment and room to breathe and expand. The benefits of connecting with our own inner light are many:

- Helping us see deeper truths
- Overcoming stuck, trapped thought patterns
- Others seeing us for who we truly are
- Channeling creativity
- Connecting to something greater than ourselves
- Knowing our place in the world and how to give back
- Improving relationships

Dancing, drumming, painting, singing, and immersing yourself in nature are other effective ways of achieving this important connection. Use the following visualization to generate a strong connection to your own inner light.

Visualization
INNER LIGHT VISUALIZATION

Allow your breathing to come to a steady pace. With each inhale and exhale, feel your body getting more and more relaxed.

Imagine a beam of light surging through your entire body, going through the top of your head connecting you with the divine, and down through the soles of your feet, connecting you with the center of the Earth.

You are always connected above and below, a column of beautiful light residing in a human body. You feel safe, grounded, and supported, like a tree with roots of light.

Continue to inhale and exhale, saying to yourself the words "relax" and "release." Notice as you breathe how the column of light surging through you expands and moves, expanding higher and higher into the cosmos.

Stay with this visualization for a few beats, recognizing your connection to all that is.

You feel connected both to yourself and to everything all at once.

Look within now, and imagine a spark of light buried deep within your heart. It might be hard to find at first, but be patient. It's there. If there's darkness around it, you may feel removed from the light inside you.

The spark is always present. Waiting for you to ignite it with care and attention.

Go into the light now and hold it, cradle it, help that light expand. Nurture your inner light, love it, allow it to grow, becoming brighter and stronger now, filling you up.

Let your own light shine, as the source of your own true power and love. Let it shine even brighter until no further barriers to that light shining remain.

Connect with your inner light. Be with it. Merge with it. Become your own inner light.

Wherever you may be on your own spiritual journey, your inner light may be dim or it may be bright. However, it's ready for you to access whenever you wish.

You are the light. You feel elevated. Ignited. Expanded. From this place of brightness you can share your light with others.

Imagine radiating your light out to those in your immediate environment. Now to your neighborhood and community. Now to the entire country, world, and universe.

Come back now to the present moment and set an intention deep within your heart that you will allow nothing or no one to dim your light.

It is there always, ready for you to shine out into the world.

CHAPTER 5

The Calming Effects of Chakra Work

Jiulio Consiglio

When you begin to work with the chakras, you're actually in the process of cultivating the mind, body, and soul, in a sense. You're working with energy, thoughts, and emotions. It's a process of digging up what's no longer serving you: old energy, limiting beliefs, and emotions that keep us stuck, or constantly stressed, in order to prepare your inner state for a more harmonious, strengthened, expanded, and balanced state of mind. The potential for experiencing a greater sense of calm is within your grasp, and it begins with having greater insight, and applying some of your intuitive nature as you go along.

Let's start by clearing up the air about a common misconception. The thoughts and emotions we experience, as well as the stresses we encounter, are not who we are but what we feel. Insight tells me that we're not separate from our outer world but one *with* it. And this is essentially demonstrated by the following: what we see out there is instantly experienced within us, and what we see regardless if it's good or bad, is reflected in our minds.

We are spiritual beings having quite the human experience. Our spiritual nature is one of peace, calm, and stillness; it's our unchangeable awareness. The authentic self, which we often hear about, is the soul or inner being. It is our true essence, who we really are, and beyond the changing nature of thoughts and emotions. The goal with these spiritual insights is to provide you with a foundation, an anchoring awareness, from which to work going forward.

Let's look closer at our thoughts and emotions through clarity so they can be better understood. Thoughts and emotions serve us in a few ways. They first offer us perspective, which is a gift. By experiencing thoughts and emotions, we can sift through our experiences and choose what we like and don't like. They also offer us contrast. Imagine how boring life would be if everyone had the same likes and dislikes. It would be like everyone wearing gray every day. Not that I don't like gray, but I want to get the message across that our differences are what add spice to life. It's the contrast that makes life exciting and enjoyable.

The next point is really important as it is an insight that will allow for the blossoming of more peace and calm in your life. It will invite the healing energy of expanded awareness. When we allow emotions and stress to bog us down and keep us stuck, it's because we have identified with these heavier energies instead of seeing them as signals from our intuitive guidance system telling us to shift ourselves back to center.

When we begin to see our thoughts, emotions, and stressors as indicators to change our focus, we will change the way we experience them. As awareness into their true purpose is welcomed, a space is created to allow relief to come into the picture. In other words, you can't fear or worry about what you understand. Our thoughts and emotions are what paint our lives on the canvas that is our awareness. What we believe and accept as true is what we give life to and what we make real. That's the creative potential we have within us.

Working with the chakras to understand how they're affected negatively and positively gives us the awareness to apply simple techniques to make positive shifts within. In this section, each chakra will be highlighted to further expand your awareness of them to reveal their connection with your state of being. In essence, this is a process that will not attempt to make you whole but rather remind you of your wholeness and completeness.

Chakra System Overview

In order to access the calming potential of the chakras, you're first going to need an understanding of the system; how it operates; and what happens energetically when a particular chakra is blocked, opened/activated, and balanced. The chakra system is composed of seven main energy wheels that begin at the base of your spine and travel upward to the top of your head. You are a mind, body, and soul, and extending from the soul is the subtle body or energetic body that houses the chakra system. The subtle body is what connects the spiritual and material, the soul and the physical body. Being the bridge between unmanifested and manifested energy, the subtle body is a reflection of its function; it's not entirely physical, nor is it entirely spiritual.

Functioning as clockwise spinning energy wheels, each chakra draws in universal energy and harnesses it to energize our entire being and transform that energy to sustain the related organs or centers pertaining to each chakra. Not only are the chakras your energy centers, but they are also responsible for the regulation of your emotional state. From a spiritual viewpoint, we're more energetic beings than physical beings. We feel, sense, react, and respond to our environments through energy, which in this case are thoughts and emotions. Approaching the chakras from this awareness empowers us and allows us to take conscious steps toward living a calmer and more peaceful life.

When one or more chakras are blocked, we may experience uneasiness, find difficulty in managing stress, and experience decreases in our overall energy. It's our thoughts and emotions that affect our chakra centers as our chakras take universal and emotional energy and translate it to the way we feel within our physical bodies. Left unchecked, accumulated emotional energy can begin to block the flow and harmony of universal energy; thereby blocking a particular chakra from functioning optimally. It's that emotional heaviness that undermines our ability to handle today's challenges or stressful situation, in a more assertive and mindful way.

As we move forward, we'll look at each chakra in particular to shed light on what feelings are experienced when a certain chakra is blocked so that you can address it and bring yourself a greater sense of calm and overall feeling of well-being. Awareness is key when you're wanting to make changes, shift your energy, empower yourself, and come into greater balance and serenity. As you become more insightful as to how you operate on a spiritual and energetic level, you will gain access to the spiritual tools and faculties required to make positive steps forward, such as forgiveness and the power of the spoken word.

When you begin the process of working with the chakras, you will start by becoming more aware of any emotional chakra blockages through the understanding of how each chakra pertains to certain feelings or emotions. As you become aware of any energetic or emotional issue, you can shed light on it, forgive, release, and let go, thereby clearing up any energetic impediment affecting the particular chakra's natural flow. As you do this, you will begin to experience a greater sense of calm and ease and start to feel lighter. You will remember how to flow and not get caught up and remain in energetic ruts. Stress will no longer rule over you but instead become a reminder to come back into alignment.

Being Grounded: Root Chakra

We're going to start with the first chakra, the root chakra, which is located at the base of the spine. Closest to the earth, this chakra anchors you and is responsible for your sense of being grounded, safe, and secure. It is the basis for all the other main chakras, and having a strong base gives you the planted sturdiness needed to work your way upward in your chakra work. When this chakra is balanced, you're able to meet challenges with greater assertiveness and confidence as it grounds you energetically. The color associated with this chakra is red.

When this chakra is blocked due to accumulated negative energy that comes from past experiences or worrying about the future, you might experience feelings of insecurity, being unable to handle stressful situations, and an overall sense that your basic needs aren't or won't be met. An imbalance in this chakra will translate to a feeling as if you're on shaky ground, so to speak. In other words, fear in one form or another is what blocks the root chakra and affects all the chakras if we're really going to get at the heart of the matter.

To begin to open and balance this chakra, you become aware of the reality of the only moment there ever is: the present. The now is the anchor. It's the rock in the sense that you can lay a strong foundation through your awareness of it and build your life in a more peaceful and calm way to move forward. The root chakra reminds me there is no calm to be found being focused on the future with its uncertainties, nor is there strength to face present day challenges dwelling on the past. This moment, this instant is where we can re-connect with our beingness and the calm waters of its essence.

As you become more aware of the present moment and grounded in its strength, you will find that your ability to handle stress will greatly improve. There is a lightness that comes with the present, a gift of higher vibrating energies that lift you up while stabilizing you and your emotions. This stabilization is accomplished in real time as you become more aligned with the main force that is found in the now—unconditional love. In other words, to ground yourself through the root chakra and present-moment awareness invites the dimension of stillness to come back to your awareness and the strength, peace, and ease it offers.

Spending time in nature, walking barefoot on grass, and hugging or placing a hand on a tree for a few minutes are excellent ways to ground yourself into the root chakra. Nature has a calming effect on us, and surrounding ourselves with Mother Nature is healing in so many ways. She reminds us to slow down, let go, and go with the flow.

Accessing Creativity and Playfulness: Sacral Chakra

The sacral chakra is the second chakra as we move upward and is located just below the navel. Representing creativity and sensuality, this chakra is the seat of artistic expression and passion. You will understand and know your self-worth, feel confident, be open to intimacy, and radiate warmth through an activated and balanced sacral chakra. Orange is the color associated with this chakra.

With an energetic imbalance, the sacral chakra reflects a loss of creativity as well as the lack of desire to express it. Relationships are affected as one feels detached from their own emotions, resulting in little interest in engaging with others. Due to an overall feeling of being unmotivated, a blocked sacral chakra will lead to experiencing a lack of passion and excitement. The person seems closed off and emotionally unavailable. Potential sources of an imbalanced sacral chakra could be a failed relationship that hasn't been forgiven and released or fear of intimacy.

In order to clear up the energy around this chakra, you're going to have to spend a little time reflecting on this chakra and narrow down the thoughts and emotions hindering its full expression. Releasing negative energy around this chakra can start with becoming aware of the belief that has created an energetic limitation or imbalance within you. Awareness is so incredibly powerful that it can dissolve negative emotion simply by your looking at it and deciding that it's no longer resonating with you. Getting in touch with your creativity by taking up a new hobby or finding something you're passionate about will also energize this chakra. Another way you can begin to heal and open this chakra is by engaging your playful side. Let go of some of the seriousness of the past and lighten up by becoming more present to start the process of freeing up this chakra energetically, which will change the way this chakra expresses itself.

As you engage with the sacral chakra and get into alignment with its energy through awareness, it will guide and assist you in clearing up its energy field. As this chakra becomes more balanced, you will feel more motivated and have a greater desire to engage with life. As the energy blockages surrounding this chakra dissolve, you'll be more open to experiencing relationships as you reflect a warm and inviting aura. Your creativity will be free to express itself through you, and that's when you'll begin to feel inspiration and open yourself up to the creative genius within all of us.

Spending time with friends and choosing to do fun things that excite you aligns you energetically with the sacral chakra. Allow your inner child to express itself, and embrace your quirkiness— it is what makes you unique. Recognizing the spontaneity of the soul to inspire and allowing it to express itself is what brings the playful side of us to the forefront of our consciousness.

Engaging Your Power: Solar Plexus Chakra

Governing your personal power, self-esteem, and independence, the solar plexus chakra, the third main chakra as we climb up the spine, is located in the stomach area. A stable solar plexus chakra provides you with the ability to approach life confidently. Coming from an awareness of inner strength and power, you are able to act courageously and live fearlessly. The color that represents this particular chakra is yellow.

If the solar plexus chakra is obstructed by negative emotion, you can be faced with feelings of helplessness, difficulty in decision-making, and an overall sense of lack of direction. Feeling stuck can also result in bouts of anger and a sense of not being in control when this chakra is not functioning optimally. Fear of moving forward or lacking the confidence to take action can make us feel closed off from our inner power. A sense of continuously repeating the past could possibly be the root cause of this chakra's imbalance.

Making conscious decisions such as healthier food choices, deciding to exercise and move the physical body consistently, and cultivating inner strength and courage by trying new things can put you on track to opening and balancing this power chakra. Becoming more aware of your power to create your reality through thoughts, words, feelings, and actions can shift you powerfully and energetically open you to new experiences with a more free-flowing solar plexus chakra. Stepping into your own authority with the awareness you can direct your life consciously in a more empowered way right here, right now, breaks the cycle of repeating the past with its lower and heavier energies, such as the belief that you are a victim of your circumstances.

The clearer the field surrounding this chakra becomes, the more you're able to deal with stress and stressful situations and draw strength and personal power from your core. As you become more self-confident and empowered to take action in your life, you'll come into alignment with your authentic self. Shifting closer to center and toward your inner being, you'll sense more of the peace and calm that already resides within you. The inner peace I'm referring to is not attached to and does not react to the outer world but is independent of it and free from conditions. The potential for such inner peace and calm is not only a potential within you; it becomes your reality when you operate from an awareness of oneness and wholeness where you are centered in mind, body, and spirit.

Opening Up: Heart Chakra

As the fourth chakra, the heart chakra is the center for unconditional love, joy, harmony, compassion, and forgiveness toward oneself and others. Its location is the center of the chest. An open and expanded heart chakra extends the wholeness of love and compassion. The experience of being in this field of awareness is one of self-acceptance and acceptance of others without con-dition. Seeing the futility of holding on to anger, one is quick to forgive themselves and others as they're reminded that to hold on to anger is to only attack oneself. Green is the color that is linked to this chakra.

When this chakra is blocked, we tend to be impeded by thoughts of anger connected to the past, hold on to grudges, refuse to forgive, and experience moments of self-hatred. Depriv-ing ourselves of peace and harmony by continuously embracing the negative emotion of anger only punishes ourselves through a conflicted heart. The contractive experience of closing others off may result in commitment issues from being in this lower vibra-tory energetic state. There is difficulty finding beauty and happi-ness in the world, as we no longer see it within ourselves. In other words, a darkened heart will give us a darkened point of view.

One of the quickest ways to heal and open the heart chakra is through forgiveness. When I say forgiveness, that includes the for-getting part, or at least being mindful that when the past attempts to remind you of what another did to you, you have the awareness that it's only the past trying to keep you stuck. Forgiving your-self and those who have caused you pain releases you. When you can release yourself of anger and the guilt that is always tied to the past, you can begin to extend forgiveness to others. You don't have to call the person and tell them you've forgiven them; you can simply do it within your mind. After all, that's where all your experiences are, within your very own consciousness. Through forgiveness, the direct experience of inner peace and calmness is invited. As negative emotion is released, we become quieter inside and allow our beingness, the soul, to shine through. It's the inner quiet that reflects the peace of the soul that offers us a renewing of our minds.

As the heart chakra is opened through forgiveness, it will begin to extend more spiritual gifts to yourself and others. You'll begin to feel more lighthearted, experience a softening of your edges, and start to radiate the unconditional love that is within you, that is you. Kindness will overflow from your state of being, and you'll see not only the beauty in life once again but also the perfection of what you've faced in the past as it led you to an expanded heart chakra. With a healed heart chakra, relationships that were once negatively affected are mended. If you're no longer sharing your life with a person who once hurt or betrayed you, you're now free of that past energy and able to start anew through a renewed and strengthened heart center.

Volunteering some of your time toward those in need is an excellent way to cultivate empathy and compassion to further expand the heart chakra. An act of kindness, even a smile, is good for the fourth chakra for it is charitable love expressing itself. A silent blessing offered to a stranger as you go about your day transforms the receiver and the one extending that kindness and love as there really are no small actions when they are heart-centered.

Expressing Yourself: Throat Chakra

Presiding over your ability to express yourself energetically and physically, the fifth or throat chakra allows you to extend its highest spiritual truths through deep awareness and understanding. Located in the throat area, you're able to communicate honestly and effectively when this chakra is operating free from fear and worry of what others think of you. When balanced, this chakra inspires creativity and authentic self-expression. The color blue is associated with this chakra.

When you're unable to express yourself authentically or feel you're being misunderstood, you may be dealing with a throat chakra that is out of alignment. Speaking negatively about others, always wanting to dominate conversations, or feeling anxious about expressing yourself are reflections of a throat chakra imbalance. The feelings associated with a blocked fifth chakra can range from thoughts of inferiority to superiority. You may appear shy and timid or overly obnoxious.

Becoming aware of how we've been expressing ourselves is the first step in bringing balance back to this chakra. Taking a step back and examining how we share our thoughts, emotions, and opinions brings awareness and clarity to how we operate. Choosing to see others through the present rather than the past, focusing on gratitude, opting to see the good in things, and speaking from a more positive mindset breaks up old, limiting energy that affects this particular chakra. Focusing on the breath to bring ourselves back to the moment invites mindfulness into our everyday lives. Letting go of the idea that we need to rush through every moment also invites balance, energetically speaking.

Working consciously with the throat chakra to become more aware of what you're putting out into the universe and how you're expressing yourself can be quite transformative. You'll find you're able to more easily relate to others, make deeper connections, and become a greater listener as this chakra comes into balance. As you become more present and engage with others, conversations will flow; allowing others to express themselves allows for more honest and authentic communication.

Other ways to bring balance to this chakra include journaling, a form of expression in which you put thoughts to paper and sit in silent meditation for a few minutes every day to practice present moment awareness. Silent meditation hones your listening skills as you place your attention on the quiet surrounding you. Present moment awareness invites clarity to make you more mindful of how you express yourself and invite fresh energy to flow through the fifth chakra.

Seeing Clearly: Third Eye Chakra

The seat of clarity, wisdom, and intuition, the sixth or third eye chakra is the commanding center that gives us spiritual sight. Located in the forehead between the eyebrows, this chakra is the doorway to your highest self and universal or cosmic consciousness, which transcends the thinking mind. This chakra is of particular importance to those who've had their fill of the emotions offered through the thinking mind, as this chakra is what connects you to the dimension of inner stillness: the unchanging and unmoving state that is a quiet or silent mind. When one is in full alignment with the sixth chakra, the direct experience is one of expanded awareness and a peace beyond words. Operating through an open and activated third eye affords you spiritual tools such as clarity, wisdom, and understanding to approach life and all of its challenges with tremendous confidence and fearlessness. It connects your conscious or local mind (the mind that is aware of its surroundings) to the unbound, non-local, limitless mind of source energy. When these minds become one, you begin to think, speak, and act from an awareness that knows its creative potential. Indigo is the color associated with this chakra.

Every chakra is always operating at a certain level, and the same goes for the brow chakra. It's not that this chakra isn't operating in and through us already, but rather it's a lack of awareness of its reality and potential that keeps the door closed to the profound insights and spiritual gifts it has to offer. With that being said, a third eye chakra blanketed by negative emotion will leave one unaware of their spiritual identity and creative power to manifest their reality. To those of us who are especially sensitive to energies or are empathic, even a partially closed third eye can make living through the thinking mind with its emotions a challenging task, to say the least.

A third eye chakra that has yet to be activated has us operating mainly between the past and future (linear time) to give us the contrast of emotions we experience such as sadness, guilt, regret, fear, worry, and uncertainty relative to our inner light of consciousness. There's nothing wrong with operating in this fashion, but problems can arise when there is an imbalance between negative and positive thoughts, negative emotions, and spiritual awareness or a lack thereof. In other words, too much of something—in this case, negativity—can further close us off from our spiritual reality and leave us not knowing ourselves at a deeper level, which prevents us from making deeper connections with others. I should also mention that being too spiritual can leave one not being able to relate to others and the challenges they're facing. In other words, balance is key.

The required spiritual work surrounding this powerful and mysterious chakra is mainly the cultivation of awareness. Awareness is everything when it comes to integrating practical and useful spirituality as well as the ability to directly experience your inner being. You can start by becoming keenly aware of the reality that is the present moment. Your spiritual nature, the authentic self, is not found in the past or future but right here and now. This instant is where the soul is encountered and where we can have a direct experience with source energy. The more you consciously align with the present, the more you will ascend in consciousness. You will lighten up and elevate your awareness beyond the thinking mind and toward the highest self, which will give you the experience of stillness and inner peace.

As you anchor your awareness into the now, you'll still able to experience the mind constructs of past and future but you may also find that as time goes by, you're less attached to them and identify with them less as you become more conscious of your eternal and spiritual nature. The closer you come to your own soul, the more you'll begin to think and speak from the present through higher dimensions of consciousness. As you shed emotional layers that have accumulated over time by being mindful of the now, the more your true self will be able to shine through. In the process, you may find you're tapping into inspiration, profound insights, and your intuition more fully, which all guide you and remind you of who you are beyond a physical body.

Another way to come into alignment with the third eye chakra is through the practice of positive affirmations, which are covered more in depth at the end of this chapter. I always find that less is more when it comes to making shifts in our lives. Spending a few minutes a day in quiet contemplation and just being present wherever you are can be incredibly transformative. It can also spark a spiritual awakening that leads to the next section, where the third eye chakra's potential becomes a possibility that allows us to have a direct experience with our own spirituality.

Spiritually Aware: Crown Chakra

Located at the top of your head and representing your connection to source energy and universal consciousness, the seventh main chakra, or crown chakra, allows you to access profound feelings of joy and bliss. The experience of a fully opened and balanced crown chakra is that of oneness. In this state, which is the return to one's beingness, we no longer identify with things like labels and judgments. We have recognized our spiritual nature and awakened from the dreaming state of thought. At this frequency or level of awareness, mystical experiences such as visions or audible messages from source energy become possible. The present is the anchoring factor as the realization is it's in the moment where the highest self is encountered. Purple is the color related to this chakra.

A closed or imbalanced crown chakra results in the desire for excess materialism due to a disconnection to one's spirituality. Because there is a void felt, the person will seek outwardly rather than within for fulfillment. In this frame of mind, there is a feeling of being separate from everything and everyone, and feelings of loneliness are not uncommon.

To begin reconnecting with the highest self and return to the feeling and awareness of oneness starts with bringing your focus and awareness inward. Life, the outer world with its challenges, and deadlines are what distracts us from recognizing the calm of inner stillness already present within us as we're too busy looking out there. As you go within and become more present within yourself, you may become aware of thoughts of old, stale, unresolved energies. Don't be afraid of them. Make the choice to observe instead of react to them, forgive them, and let them go. As you take this mental action of observing and witnessing your automatic thoughts, you'll invite greater awareness into the picture. As greater awareness is allowed to blossom, you'll start to align more with the authentic self and the healing energies it is always offering.

Realizing that separation is an illusion and everything and everyone is connected on an energetic level takes new sight, and is offered through an activated third eye that sees oneness. No one can convince you of this; it's something that has to be experienced directly and through the awareness of inner stillness when there is no thought. A quiet mind, in other words. To be clear, inner stillness is universal consciousness or cosmic consciousness. It is the all-encompassing awareness found in every reality, everything, and everyone. In stillness, all thoughtforms dissolve. When thought disappears, it's replaced by presence, awareness, and peace.

Chakra Balancing for Calmness

I've always found that simple and straightforward practices and exercises for making shifts in our lives and bringing personal change—in this case, a greater sense of calm—are most effective. In this section, I'm going to introduce a simple and effective exercise that only takes minutes but can achieve amazing results. Let's begin.

Balance and Calmness Exercise

The first and most important thing I want to mention before we move into the exercise is the powerful and life-affirming phrase "I AM." When we utter those words, we ignite universal forces here and now, not sometime in the future. You become what you think or say when it begins with "I AM" on an energetic level, which is then translated into physical reality. With that idea in mind, let's move forward and address each chakra to assist you in coming into greater balance and harmony.

Find a quiet space and get comfortable. Eyes can be open or closed. Take a few breaths and become aware of the moment and the present. Drop your shoulders and just be.

Address the particular chakra you want to work with, or all of them, by speaking out loud with confidence and feeling, each of the phrases that pertain to the certain chakra three times. As you're affirming for a particular chakra, envision in your mind the color that pertains to it, freely turning clockwise as a circle of energy in the area where the chakra is located.

These are the affirmations, colors, and location for reference:

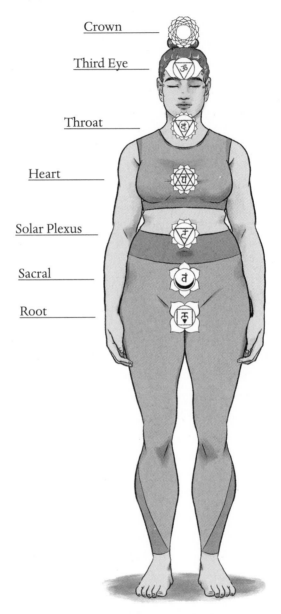

Crown

Third Eye

Throat

Heart

Solar Plexus

Sacral

Root

Map of Chakras on the Body

Root Chakra: "I am grounded in the present." "I am safe, and secure always."
Color: red
Location: base of spine

Sacral Chakra: "I am creative." "I am playful, and sexy."
Color: orange
Location: below navel

Solar Plexus Chakra: "I am powerful." "I am strong and confident."
Color: yellow
Location: stomach

Heart Chakra: "I am unconditional love." "I am kindness and compassion."
Color: green
Location: center of chest

Throat Chakra: "I am honest and authentic." "I am speaking my truth."
Color: blue
Location: throat area

Third Eye Chakra: "I am connected to my intuition." "I am aligned with clarity."
Color: indigo
Location: forehead, between eye brows

Crown Chakra: "I am joy, bliss and happiness." "I am one with infinite intelligence and wisdom."

Color: purple

Location: top of head (because of this chakra's location, envision purple energy swirling clockwise that radiates upward from the top of your head)

This exercise can be done daily or a few times a week, as it only takes a few minutes. You are the best gauge as to how you're feeling. Remember to allow your inner guidance system to assist you while you work with the chakras and practice this exercise. Pay attention and listen to the cues about when you need to affirm these powerful statements. Once you're done with the exercise, take a few deep breaths, give thanks that what you desire is done, and let the moment go. The last thing I want to mention is that these statements need belief behind them. To go a step further, they require knowing. You need to know that what you desire is what source desires for you, and you need to know that what you speak and think becomes your reality. That's the power that dwells within us, and it's only potential until it's recognized, honored, and activated through belief, but even more so, knowing.

Chakra Maintenance

Maintaining balanced chakras is in essence a moment-by-moment process. Living through the present moment understandably requires spiritual awareness, which is not how we as human beings have been taught to approach life. Our human conditioning has come with contrast, duality, and the belief in linear time: past, present, and future. It is living solely through the past and future without much examination or awareness of the present that created the emotional density that has blanketed our consciousness and energetically affected our chakras to make life more challenging.

But through awareness, recognizing the tool that is our conscious mind and our power to call forth and manifest our reality, we can bring back balance within ourselves as we reclaim our power through the authentic self. Keep in mind that nothing has to be added to you. You have to let go and release what no longer serves you while allowing your spiritual gifts and intuition to guide you back to the peace and calm that is your very own essence: the soul.

CHAPTER 6

Astrology and
Self-Care

Leah Patterson

Astrology and self-care might not seem like a natural fit, but since we see astrology as a tool to better understand ourselves, why not take it further and see it as the potent tool it can be in taking better care of ourselves? With astrology at the helm, you can find self-care practices to truly fit you. This chapter will help you craft a uniquely beautiful brand of self-care that changes as we change and truly fills our cup with exactly what we need. When you use astrology as your guide, you can make sense of all the beautiful, magical self-care rituals available and blend them in a way that soothes, mends, and rejuvenates your unique soul.

Early on in my life, I was fascinated by astrology. It presented the key to who I was. It helped me be okay with me and explained how I ticked and why. As I delved deeper into astrology, so much clicked and made sense. It was as though I found the missing part to understanding myself.

I didn't realize the connection between astrology and self-care until much later. From an early age, I suffered from anxiety and depression while fully functioning as a high-achieving, goal-oriented, force to be reckoned with. My life consisted of pushing myself hard, people-pleasing, and comparing myself to anyone and everyone. What was worse is that I was barely conscious of it. I trudged through life in cycles of highs and lows without realizing how much of it was my own doing. I definitely was not aware I could actively do anything about it. It wasn't until I learned about this wonderful thing called self-care that I began to lift my head from the fog that had been bogging my life down for so long. Self-care gave me the permission and the pause I needed to begin changing my experience of life. Over time, I began to use astrology and its knowledge to help ease my anxiety, calm my worrying mind, and give me the break I sometimes needed from life, ultimately rejuvenating and recharging me.

Self-care was such a turning point, because I learned I didn't have to rely on anyone else to approve of, love, affirm, or even care for me. I learned I could do all those things for myself and probably better than anyone. Before I learned this, I always looked for approval and love outside of myself and subconsciously expected others to fill my cup and help me feel better about life. I secretly resented loved ones and friends because they couldn't automatically see when I needed a break or some extra love and didn't swoop in to save me.

Self-care is what gave me my own wings and the power to save myself. Learning to fill my own cup is what set me free from the pits of despair of anxiety and depression. It was that monumental for me, and it can be that monumental for you too!

Why Is Self-Care So Important?

Maybe you're like me: super driven, Jacqueline of all trades, always thinking of new ideas, always on the go. When you live that life and never make time to take care of yourself, burnout is an inevitable result. With that burnout, feelings of letting yourself down are not far behind. You cycle between pushing and striving and inevitably crashing and burning.

This sad cycle repeats for good reason. With all those dreams you have and ideas you're planning to see through, it's hard to make good on them when you're burnt out and running on empty. Self-care cleanses and fills your tank back up.

Maybe you're a person who lives in your mind. You don't have a great connection with your body and spend a lot of time thinking about great things but rarely doing them. You get excited about all the things you're planning to do but somehow never get around to them. You muse about how awesome this and that might be but never make time for it. You beat yourself up for all of it and wonder why. It's not that you're forever flawed; you just haven't been filling your cup and fueling yourself effectively. Self-care is the type of fuel that fills your cup and with the right type of fuel. This fuel gives you the energy you need to see those dreams and great plans becoming a reality.

Or maybe you're someone who is stuck in a loop of comparison, constantly comparing yourself to others, doubting yourself, and trying to please everyone along the way. Self-care gives you the space to actually see your worth and actively express it. When you spend enough time actively expressing your worth by showing yourself how worthy you are through action, you'll find it easier to assert yourself, your boundaries, and your awesomeness.

Without an active practice of self-care, you can find yourself on a slippery slope to compounding depression and anxiety. You are weary and excessively hard on yourself, beating yourself up over things outside of your control and struggling to keep a positive outlook and the motivation to keep going.

You might ask, "But isn't it enough to get others to approve of me?" It's true that you might get a boost of external inspiration that temporarily boosts your mood, but it's inevitably short-lived. You'll eventually find yourself right back in that pit of malaise, feeling worse off than before. You need to break the cycle, and refueling with self-care is what does it.

Self-care recharges you. It's the number one thing that gives you the ability to do anything else. That may sound like a bold statement, but read on and I'm sure you'll begin to agree with me. Self-care is the fuel we need to nurture ourselves and provide our minds, bodies, and spirits with the nutrients needed to flourish.

When it comes to our bodies, providing the nutrients and exercise needed to physically thrive is a well-known and accepted truth, but even this is something we often fail at. However, that's not the case with our minds and spirits. We rarely prioritize the care they need to flourish. Honestly, mind- and spiritwise, we can really drop the ball.

Think about those moments when you have taken the time to do a little something for yourself. You've slowed down enough to savor the moment. You've given yourself an extra treat. You've indulged in something you normally wouldn't make time for. Remember how rejuvenated and energized it felt and how suddenly you had more energy and inspiration than you did just a bit ago? That's the magic of self-care.

How to Make Self-Care Be More than Superficial

Sometimes the self-care we choose doesn't do it for us and we are left wondering why. A platitude or general suggestion scratches at our need for self-care, and so we try it. We think it's replenishing us when in reality, it just becomes one more thing to do, empty of any real lasting value. It feels shallow and we don't truly feel rejuvenated from the core at the end of it. You may feel okay at best, checking a box on your to-do list. Or worse, you may feel like you've wasted time and find yourself more turned off of making that time for yourself again in the future.

How can you avoid that feeling, especially when you're new to self-care principles? Here is where astrology shines as your worthy guide! Astrology can help you find the self-care principles and techniques that will work deeply for you, replenish your unique soul, and rejuvenate your unique spirit.

Modalities and Elements Lead the Way

A powerful way to use your astrological signs to discover the self-care practices best suited to you is understanding each sign's modalities and elements. Each sun sign has a particular modality and element associated with it to give the sign a particular energy. The modality and elements of a sign shine a light on the broad strokes by which groups of signs can be identified. These components give you further insight into the characteristics of a sign as well as the motivations that drive it, the places where it gets weary and needs replenishment, and the spaces it naturally thrives in. Specifically, the modalities give a sense of a sign's behavior and adaptability. The elements give a sense of a sign's temperament and overall way of thinking. We can use the modalities and elements to carve out a self-care practice unique to us.

There are three modalities and four elements. The three modalities are mutable, fixed, and cardinal. Think of them as similar to the changing of the seasons: cardinal is at the beginning of the season, fixed is the middle, and mutable at the end. The modalities give you an idea of what things naturally lighten your energy and ways you might drain your energy and need it replenished.

Mutable signs are most tuned to transformation and adaptability since they appear toward the end of a season when it is changing to the next one. This modality prepares for change, is open to opinions, and is ready to shift when the time comes.

Being in the middle, fixed signs have the energy of staying power. They coincide with the flourishing time of a season when that season's energy is at its peak. They have the most static, grounded energy of the modalities. This translates to reliability, loyalty, and stubbornness. Ultimately, their energy can always be depended on.

Cardinal signs are the starters. They have the energy of rapid change, quick thinking, and initiation. Being at the start of every season, their energy is geared toward setting things in motion. They have the focus necessary to see something start from nothing, creating the spark and driving the push into new experiences, full steam ahead.

The four elements are earth, air, fire, and water. Each element has innate personality traits given to its sign group. The elements give you a sense of what you naturally gravitate toward in addition to spaces and practices that you find most comforting and replenishing.

Earth signs have a slow and steady nature. They have an appreciation for things that can be seen and touched and have a deeply sensual side. The most grounded signs of the zodiac, they gravitate toward logic and sensibility. Often, beauty soothes and rejuvenates them.

Air signs are seen as the least grounded signs of the zodiac. They can be the least outwardly emotional and tend to find their comfort in the intellect through conversation and deep thinking. Curious by nature, they love learning new things and sharing their ideas and are always seeking out connection and knowledge. Conversation and connection soothe them.

Fire signs are the initiators of the zodiac. Their energy is spontaneous, impulsive, and inspiring. They typically move to the beat of their own drum and are natural born leaders who engage others through inspiring action and example. They often have big ideas and lots of passion to get them going. Creativity is what soothes them.

Water signs are the emotional set points of the zodiac. Water signs teach us about our emotions, as they are the signs most in touch with them and the most comfortable navigating them. These signs are natural nurturers and have an ability to handle the depths of the happiness and sorrows of others. Emotional cleansing soothes these signs.

Next, we'll look at the self-care needs of each modalitiy and element and explore how to combine that knowledge and create a self-care plan.

Self-Care Needs of Modalities

The mutable signs—Gemini, Virgo, Sagittarius, and Pisces—are typically plagued by their duality and ability to be so flexible and adaptable. This can make them verge on flighty in the case of Gemini and Pisces or overcompensate into rigidity as tends to be the case with Sagittarius and Virgo. What will soothe them best is a brief reprieve from high-stakes decision making. What will replenish them is participating in philosophical thought and/or light-hearted activities that allow them to experiment, explore multiple outcomes, and engage just for the sake of engaging.

The fixed signs are Taurus, Leo, Scorpio, and Aquarius. They are typically plagued by over-indulgence and stagnant energy. It's important for these signs to regularly detox from intensity and engage in movement and quick action. These signs can fixate and cause a state of worry that paralyzes them. Finding ways to break unhealthy hyper-focus and lighten their energy (typically through physical play like exercise, dance, and sports) will do wonders for replenishing these signs.

The cardinal signs—Aries, Cancer, Libra, and Capricorn—are generally so highly activated they need to lean into relaxation and rest. These signs tend to have a lot of built-up energy that needs to be discharged and released. Learning how to rest and calm their nervous systems will make the difference with these signs and help them restore their balance.

Self-Care Needs of Elements

When the air signs—Gemini, Libra, and Aquarius—are out of balance, they typically are out of touch with their emotions and triggered into an emotionally detached and aloof space. Deescalating and reconnecting on a safe emotional level is important to destress and recharge air signs. Finding a trusted friend to engage in a mutual activity is a great way to do this. Connection is the most important point here, as air signs can isolate themselves and spiral into more dysfunction.

The water signs—Cancer, Scorpio, and Pisces—need a break from their emotions when they are out of balance. They need to be able to ease up on taking whatever situation, thought, or thing so seriously and find play and lightheartedness in it. A good dose of healthy detachment is good for water signs. Realizing they aren't responsible for the emotional state of all things is a very important self-care mantra for them.

The earth signs—Taurus, Virgo, and Capricorn—need a step out of seriousness as well. Earth signs can become fixated on something to the point where they stagnate their own energy and drain themselves. These signs need to lean into their physicality and get active to break up stagnant energy and bring different perspectives and ideas to the surface.

The fire signs—Aries, Leo, and Sagittarius—are generally overstimulated when out of balance. They need to find calm. Being in soothing, nonactive environments will give their adrenals a rest and allow them to recharge at leisure. Mindfulness activities that allow them to focus on one thing at a time will help these signs to find peace within their fiery energy of activation.

Using Modalities and Elements to Choose Self-Care Activities

Now that you have an understanding of how the modalities and elements work, you can begin to use these combos to fine-tune your self-care practices. For instance, if your sun sign is Capricorn, you're a cardinal earth sign. This means that on your best days, you have a spark of innovation to begin something new and the wherewithal to see it through. On your worst day, you might drive yourself to endlessly work and never feel satisfaction in what you're doing because you're always striving toward the next new thing. To really replenish your spirit, you might take a staycation at a local spa and opt for a full body massage and facial. With these choices, you can lean into relaxation and enjoy the physical sensations of the body and face treatments.

Let's take a look at the tendencies of each sign and take into account the modalities and elements for crafting self-care practices.

Aries–Cardinal/Fire

Aries are the babies of the zodiac, which can be a blessing and a curse. Aries energy is fresh and new. It's always ready to jump into a new adventure. It's bright, bold, and at times all-consuming. Some might even say it's arrogant and impulsive. This impulsive energy is the stuff of audacious beginnings. Aries energy is the small spark of life that grows into the blazing flame over time. It must plow ahead, full force in the early stages of anything. It must be ready to say yes and forge new paths at the drop of a hat. For this reason, Aries needs moments of calm and recharge.

Self-care for Aries looks like slowing down and mentally and physically taking a break from initiating. Even though initiating is what Aries does best, they also need experience not being first. Aries needs to be able to relax into the knowing that not every good idea needs to be seen through. Aries needs to also realize the benefit of wise counsel—they don't have to bear the full weight of being the initiator or always choose what happens next.

Looking at the modality and element of Aries, it makes sense that Aries are the initiators. The modality of cardinal and element of fire give Aries a double-whammy of starter energy. Because of this, Aries needs help to discharge that activated energy when in need of rebalancing. A perfect method of self-care for Aries is to engage in a noncompetitive physical activity with a friend. Crafting, dancing, or sports are examples of perfect fits; doing something physical allows an Aries to engage their body while rejuvenating their mind and helps them tap into their creativity and get recharged.

Taurus—Fixed/Earth

Taurus energy is slow, steady, determined, and at times immovable. Taurus sits strong in their convictions and lives in and for the moment. This is why Taurus is also the sign of indulgence and opulence. Taureans generally love a good party. They have a strong sense of commitment and can be seen as stubborn at times, as their commitment can sometimes be short-sighted and hard to shift. They can use that same bull-headed tenacity to hold fast to an ideal and fight for a cause.

What Taurus needs to replenish themselves is healthy indulgence. They need to lighten their burdens of commitment and allow themselves the fun of play but within limits. Because overindulgence is one of their vices, self-care could look like choosing healthy, fulfilling foods and activities—ones that give back instead of deplete.

Modality- and element-wise, we're looking at fixed earth. On a great day, Taurus has the ability to stay the course and build something great. On a stressed day, Taurus can find themselves maxed out and feeling weighed down and jaded. Taurus needs to be reinspired by the beauty of life again and coaxed to re-engage. Indulging in brunch at a great restaurant with an inspiring friend is one perfect way to do this. Their senses will be piqued, and they'll find in the conversation reason to step back into the fray of intentional work again.

Gemini—Mutable/Air

Gemini is the sign of communication and duality. Gemini energy is both-sided, able to see and understand all perspectives. They have an uncanny ability to be the center of attention, communicating with ease with anyone and everyone, sometimes overstepping boundaries, and all the time making others completely okay with it in the process. Their ability to charm others and synthesize tons of information is uncanny.

Because they are typically taking in tons of sensory input, Gemini needs to be able to shut it down and shut it off to recharge. They need to be in a space where they can control the sensory input and calm their minds.

Modality- and element-wise, Gemini's mutable air gives Gemini the ability to always see the other side of things and continuously be on the cutting edge of new ideas and ways of thinking. However, having a brain that's always buzzing can become exhausting. What can bring them peace is engaging in mindfulness and meditative practices. Finding a favorite guided meditation in particular will help this sign to calm, center, and focus while dissipating the agitated energy that can come from thinking a million thoughts in succession, sometimes all at once.

Cancer—Cardinal/Water

Cancers are the nurturers of the zodiac. They can easily feel the emotions of others and get lost in their own emotions as well. Their energy is outwardly focused on others within their circle. They are the ones who mother and care for everyone, sometimes to their own detriment. Cancers are therefore the emotional backbone of their communities, attending to the needs of their chosen family and applying their natural tendency to create comfort and security.

Out of balance, Cancerian energy can become manipulative and smothering. Cancers can find themselves feeling overly paranoid about how their chosen family feels about them and can compensate for that through moodiness and/or clinginess. This is especially the case if they are still maturing in age and emotional intelligence. Cancerian energy goes deep. They are the protectors of hearth and home, carrying the torch that passes down family traditions and tending to the fibers that create and maintain the depth of our core relationships.

Cancers have the modality and elemental combination of cardinal water. This gives them the power to sway the emotional state of others and be the biggest influence in the room, so to speak. When in balance, they use this big energy to create nurturing, warm spaces and a sense of security and safety for their people. They are able to tune in to the exact needs of their collective and delight in fulfilling them. When out of balance, Cancers may become manipulative with their influential energy, using their emotional nurturing as a bargaining chip to force others to be the recipients. This stems from insecurities that creep up when Cancers are overextended. What helps them rebalance and recenter is engaging in activities that allow them to turn that nurturing ability inward and create a safe space for themselves. A great example of this is treating themselves to a special treat they've made that would normally be given away. Taking a moment to ask their inner child what they would like to do today and then clearing their schedule and fully engaging in that is another great way. Activities like these will help Cancers fill their own cup so they can get back to pouring into others.

Leo—Fixed/Fire

Leo energy is all about showing up. It's the energy of audacious courage, bold gestures, and great fanfare. Leos don't shy away from being at the center and letting everyone see them. Leos tend to take the role of protectors of their chosen family and pride themselves on being dependable and inspiring leaders for their people. They can be warm and generous and have a natural ability to instill a sense of comfort and ease. People feel safe and supported by them.

Out of balance, Leo energy can become desperate for the spotlight and can vie for it by any means necessary. They carry an immense amount of pressure to be seen as impeccable in the public eye, to always have the right answer, and to always know the best path forward. Because of this, Leo energy can become harsh, overbearing, and cold. They'd rather hide their unsureness than let it be seen, lest it be seen as a weakness.

Leo energy has the modality and element combination of fixed fire. This combination generates a tenacious spirit of excitement and motivation. On its best day, a Leo can motivate a crowd of naysayers to take on a new path with them as their leader. But on their worst day, a Leo sign can take drastic measures to be the chosen one without caring who gets caught in the fray, a tendency that stems from insecurity and moodiness. When a Leo is out of balance, those voices can get louder. To bring back balance, Leos can engage in activities that boost their confidence while dispersing the riled-up fire energy in creative ways. Solving logic puzzles/brain teasers like Sudoku can do this, as can taking up a creative arts class like painting or drawing. In this way, Leos can use their innate creativity and lean into their confidence without it being high-stakes.

Virgo—Mutable/Earth

Virgo energy is all about purification, perfection, and systems. It thrives on being able to analyze and organize life and often finds comfort in dedicating to a pursuit, giving it the proper time, attention, and focus to see it through to its end. Virgos have the ability to apply themselves in very logical, practical, and precise ways and often feel like they are the only ones who can do a task the right way. They have a penchant for efficiency and don't appreciate fluff.

Self-care for Virgos looks like releasing anxiety and worry. Virgos can sometimes get so caught up in minor details that they work themselves into a frenzied state that's hard to break free from. Finding ways to lighten up and engage in play does wonders for rejuvenating and recharging them.

As a mutable earth sign, Virgos can be adaptable and dependable. The combination of transformative energy coupled with the grounded earth energy gives Virgos a unique ability to choose impactful, inspirational tasks that they also have the tenacity to see through. Out of balance, this energy can become too unsettled and rigid. Finding inspiring work is what will get Virgos back in balance. A small but important task will recharge their systems and get them back in flow.

Libra—Cardinal/Air

Libra is the great balancer. Libran energy is about keeping the peace and bringing harmony to all things. Libran energy wants to see things in balance and flowing with the warm feel-good energy of synchronicity. Because of their desire to be an instigator of peace, Libras have a natural charisma and charm. They are kind, considerate, and sympathetic to the needs of others and do their best to meet them.

When Libras find themselves out of balance, it's often a symptom of losing themselves in attempting to find the common ground for others. Libras may find it hard to make decisions and can struggle more than others when there's underlying stress or general tension among their friend groups. They can also be insincere; their desire to please overpowers their ability to be honest about their feelings. To replenish themselves, Libras need time away from pleasing others and specifically time alone to get back in touch with themselves and their own desires.

Modality- and element-wise, Libras are cardinal air. They have the ability to ignite their charm and create great bonds through conversation and mutual interests. However, when they are out of balance, they can find themselves overly stimulated and feeling detached from their community. Their minds can run rampant and prey on their insecurities about making sure everyone is happy and can cause them to retreat. In order to calm these insecurities and find peace of mind again, this sign benefits from solo activities like a luxurious bath or a meditative solo picnic, where they can delight in their senses and not be bogged down by thinking of anyone else for a change.

Scorpio—Fixed/Water

Scorpio energy is related to the depth of emotions, carrying the energy of the shadow and the heavier sides of life. This gives Scorpios the ability to handle and transmute heavy emotions, something they often do for their loved ones. They feel more comfortable than any other sign grappling with life's darkest aspects, and they have the rare perspective to be able to find beauty in that darkness. They have a natural resilience and dedication along with a sincere sensitivity.

Out of balance, Scorpio energy can become manipulative and possessive. They can use their comfort with depth to overpower others, and if they get stuck in the depths of their own emotions, they can become jaded and stagnant. In order to break up that energy and get the deep waters of the Scorpio temperament flowing again, they need to engage in activities that spark hope and inspiration. Spending time listening to motivational videos or uplifting music can make a world of difference for this sign.

Looking at its modality and element, we find fixed water. In good spirits, Scorpio can be the emotional support for their friend group. They have the resilience and staying power to lead by example and patiently guide. When out of balance, however, Scorpios can drown themselves and those close to them with heaviness. To lighten this energy and give themselves the release they need, detoxing treatments can do the trick. Engaging in a one-day physical fast or spending the weekend at a silent retreat are two ways to cleanse their emotional palate and create space for their peace of mind.

Sagittarius—Mutable/Fire

Sagittarius is the great wanderer of the zodiac. Sagittarians have the ability to be at home anywhere and carry an inner sense of comfort with them at all times. Out of all the signs, they are the most comfortable in their skin. This gives them an inner confidence that doesn't necessarily exude but is hard to miss all the same. Being a fire sign, they are enthusiastic about life, adventurous, and energetic. The flipside is that they are uncomfortable sitting still too long and have a hard time with processing heavy emotions. They'd much rather get distracted by the next exciting thing.

When Sagittarius needs self-care, they, like Scorpios, need to be re-inspired about life. When out of balance, they isolate themselves and harshly push away their loved ones. Self-care looks like finding joy again for Sagittarius. Sagittarians need to inject their life with passion and excitement to find their natural stride again.

As a mutable fire sign, Sagittarius energy is adaptable and fiery. The innate passion for life that Sagittarians have makes sense in this light. When this sign is shining, its zest and boundlessly energetic wanderlust inspires even the most conservative and melancholy. When out of balance however, Sagittarian energy can become over-stimulated and exhausted or even worse—uninspired and apathetic. Something as simple as setting aside time to read an inspiring novel is a great way to reset and one that Sagittarians would especially appreciate.

Capricorn—Cardinal/Earth

Capricorns are one of the most steadfast, hard-working signs of the zodiac. They have a natural tenacity and practicality that sees them choosing worthwhile pursuits and putting in the work to see them through. In fact, Capricorns won't waste their time on anything that doesn't have tried-and-true promise in their eyes. Capricorns are also achievement seekers and will place almost everything behind the quest to excel.

Self-care for Capricorns is about helping them lighten up and remember the little bits of joy and happiness of life. Out of balance, Capricorns can become rigid and overly focused on achieving. They can become cold and unable to see the value in their relationships, only the collected accolades.

Being a cardinal earth sign, Capricorn's ability to push to accomplish new successes is a natural trait. They have the starter energy of a cardinal sign combined with the staying power of an earth sign. This gives them the determination and wherewithal to work hard and stick with the plan they've laid out. To keep this energy balanced, however, Capricorns need to make time to nurture their relationships as well as lean into life's less material rewards. Spending time with a cherished family member or friend enjoying an activity that both appreciate is a wonderful way for Capricorns to recharge.

Aquarius—Fixed/Air

Aquarius is considered the most individualistic sign of the zodiac. They thrive when marching to the beat of their own drums. They also are the most altruistic of the signs. Aquarians feel called to crusade for their fellow human and can often find themselves taking up social justice causes and humanitarian pursuits. This energy is also eccentric and generally considered ahead of its time. For this reason, Aquarians can feel out of touch with everyday life and unable to connect to others on a personal level. Out of balance, their energy can become extreme and detached. Their familiarity with being different from others can turn into a condescending attitude that covers up feelings of loneliness and awkwardness.

Self-care for Aquarians is about finding a connection to their humanness again. They need experiences that will help them find common ground with others and ease up on the need to be crusading. Joining a Meetup group or other small gathering of people is a great way to do this.

As a fixed air sign, Aquarius thrives at holding space for truth, novel ideas, and innovation. On a great day, Aquarius has the inquisitive nature and stability to happen upon new thoughts that can stand the test of time. Out of balance, however, Aquarian energy can become too detached and cerebral, out of touch with current reality. To restore balance, this sign needs to embrace everything that makes them feel their humanness. Eating nourishing foods, engaging with small friend groups, and doing inner child work are all great ways for Aquarians to get back in touch with what it is to be human.

Pisces—Mutable/Water

Pisces is considered the deepest sign of the zodiac. Being at the end of the zodiac, Pisceans can be said to hold the energy of all the other signs. They have an empathetic and receptive nature and are considered the most psychic. Because they are so tuned in to the emotional states of others, they can find themselves over-flooded with emotional inputs. They can tend toward martyr complexes and put others' needs well before their own, forgetting that they also require care and support. This imbalance can well up and cause Pisceans to do a disappearing act, completely retreating when emotional energy is too much for them to handle.

To recharge and rebalance, a Pisces does well by reconnecting with their own depths and putting boundaries up to separate their own emotions from others. Alone time helps Pisces find their center again, as does as partaking in creative, artistic hobbies. Creativity helps them express and dissipate built up emotional energy.

Looking at the modality / element nature of Pisces as a mutable water sign, it makes sense that Pisces have the ability to handle the emotional depths of others. Being a mutable sign gives Pisces an adaptable and transformative nature. On a great day, Pisces is able to selflessly absorb others' problems and offer assistance and support. Out of balance, however, mutable water can become overwhelmed and bogged down by the swell of others' emotions. A balancing choice for this sign is engaging in silent meditation, morning walks, and rejuvenating baths. Each of these activities can help them release and recharge.

———

Now that you have this knowledge in hand, I encourage you to make use of it right away. Take ten minutes at the beginning of each week and check in with yourself. Are you in need of some self-care? If the answer is yes, apply your newly acquired deeper understanding of yourself to craft self-care moments throughout your week that will truly replenish you. Enjoy!

CHAPTER 7

CREATING CALM THROUGH YOUR VAGUS NERVE

Cyndi Dale

When I was emotionally distraught or physically ill, my dad used to say, "One person's stress is another's opportunity." This typical Norwegian comment only made me feel worse. I would continue to struggle with the initial problem while feeling totally stupid. Why could I not turn the proverbial lemons into lemonade? I watched my dad for clues. I failed to perceive how his solution—the drinking of two or three martinis every night—served him in the long haul. Turns out, there is a real recipe for "making lemonade." It involves interacting with a singular nerve that runs throughout your physical body. This is your vagus nerve.

The vagus nerve is a hot topic in medical and scientific communities. It is one of twelve cranial nerves, yet it's by far the most important. It is involved in nearly every aspect of health and holds the key to recovering from stress and trauma. You could even call it your "serenity" nerve, if not your "sanity" nerve.

I've been researching the vagus nerve for years and am thrilled to discuss it here. I've been dedicated to improving the lives of people through my intuitive healing consultations, writings, and teachings for over three decades, and have found that interacting with the vagus nerve can ensure significant relief for nearly every sort of stress or problem.

First, I'll describe this all-important nerve, mainly from a biological perspective. I'll then offer a synopsis of energy and the two types that are involved in all aspects of your life, which are physical or measurable and subtle or spiritual. Next, I'll provide a few stories to show you how your vagus nerve can be accessed through both types of energy. I'll then present exercises including one to show you how to benefit from your intuition, to soothe your stressed-out self through your vagus nerve. These will include physical and subtle techniques, both aimed at turning those tumultuous moments into as much tranquility as possible.

What Is Your Vagus Nerve?

Your vagus nerve is one of twelve cranial nerves in your body, all of which exit from or near your upper neck. Your vagus nerve is arguably the most notable, however, because it assists with just about every aspect of your health, including the physical and psychological.

This nerve is extraordinarily long reaching, and its jobs are truly all-encompassing. Running from the left and right sides of your brain to your heart, its branches continue their downward journey to engage most other major organs. Exceptionally busy, it controls multiple life functions, like those related to digestion, cardiovascular performance, and the immune system. It also reflects the programming that determines many of your emotional reactions to events, therefore impacting your mood and feelings.

This nerve is highly interactive with your autonomic nervous system, which manages involuntary actions like the beating of your

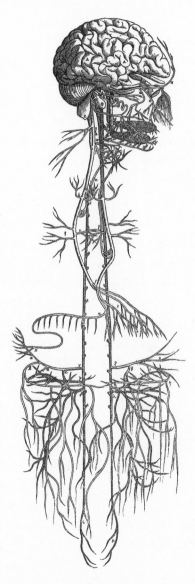

Vagus Nerve

heart and the flexibility of your blood vessels. There are three main parts of this system: the sympathetic, parasympathetic, and enteric nervous systems; in fact, your vagus nerve ties them all together.

Bear with me for the science lesson. It will reveal why interacting with your vagus nerve can help you conquer many of your worries—and open you to life's wonders.

Overall, the sympathetic nervous system's main job is to help you adjust to stress, defined as any type of internal or external stimulus that jostles you from a balanced to an imbalanced state. When it registers danger, this system creates a flash flood of anxiety-producing hormones and other chemicals, leaving you with a rapid heartbeat, quick breathing, and other stress reactions. The sympathetic system's kissing cousin is the parasympathetic nervous system, which is the primary relaxing and decompressing part of your autonomic system. If the sympathetic system is the fight and flight regulator, the parasympathetic is the rest and digest.

Your vagus nerve interacts with both parts of the sympathetic and parasympathetic systems, but about 75 percent of it is made of parasympathetic nerve fibers.[1] That means regulating your vagus nerve is a critical component of getting chill after you're hot and bothered. Plus, soothing that nerve during the moment of stress might even stop an overreaction in its tracks.

The third major player in your autonomic nervous system is your enteric nervous system, which is sometimes called the gut brain or second brain.

Your enteric system is so complex that it's almost indescribable. But we'll go for it because it explains so much about our relationship with stress. The enteric is basically a collection of different

---

1. Cleveland Clinic, "Vagus Nerve." https://my.clevelandclinic.org/health/body/22279-vagus-nerve#:~:text=The%20vagus%20nerve%2C%20also%20known,can't%20consciously%20control%20them.

types of neurons that extend from your esophagus to your rectum. While they aid in your digestion, the health of these neurons is critical for determining your basic health. That's because about 80 percent of your immune cells live in this gut brain, mainly in your intestines, which hosts between 30 and 400 trillion microbes. And these microbes are implicated in not only digestion and immunity but also your moods—such as stress reactions.[2]

Your enteric nervous system is quite profound, even as a structure. For instance, if you were to spread its neurons as a line on the ground, they would stretch 30 feet.[3] That's because there are between 400 and 600 million of these neurons, about the same number in your spine.[4] Speaking of which, your spine and brain constantly network with your enteric system to regulate everything from hunger to feelings. And what player makes sure that your gut and head brains keep up this incessant exchange of data? That's right: your vagus nerve.

Though your vagus nerve keeps your head and gut brain in constant communication, it is mainly a superhighway for what's happening in the enteric. That's because 80 to 90 percent of its nerve fibers relay data upward rather than downward.[5] Because of this, that gut brain reigns supreme. When an event triggers you, your gut will rule, no matter how hard you try to think your way out of panic.

---

2. Andrew Holmes and Dr. Carly Rosewarne, guest reviewers, "Gut bacteria: the inside story." Australian Academy of Science. https://www.science.org.au/curious/people-medicine/gut-bacteria.

3. Amber J. Tresca, "The Anatomy of the Enteric Nervous System." verywell health, February 22, 2021, https://www.verywellhealth.com/enteric-nervous-system-5112820.

4. Mark A. Fleming et al., "The Enteric Nervous System and Its Emerging Role as a Therapeutic Target." *Gastrocenterology Research and Practice*, September 8, 2020, https://www.ncbi.nlm.nih.gov/pmc/articles/PMC7495222/.

5. "Vagus Nerve," Physiopedia, https://www.physio-pedia.com/Vagus_Nerve.

What really determines how your gut brain will react to events in your life? Well, there are a lot of factors. During conception, you were imprinted with beliefs and judgments, emotional programs, and behavioral patterns from your ancestors and parents; most likely you also brought in the same through your soul, which I believe has lived before. We're all heavily influenced by our family of origin and immediate caretakers during childhood, in addition to the events we've experienced beyond our youth. Who can even pinpoint all the unconsciously acquired perceptions taken on from their culture, gender and/or sexual orientation, spirituality, ethnicity, and other influences? This mishmash and conglomerate of less-than-ideal presumptions program all aspects of our autonomic system, especially the enteric, to "tell" us what stressors are dangerous. If Grandma thought a train was scary, we might too—and we won't even know why we're scared to ride the railway.

There is yet another wellspring of traits that trigger stress responses: trauma. Trauma is stress that fails to clear. A sense of urgency is often the result of an excruciating wound that remains as an imprint, only to cause an instant reaction. For instance, I was attacked by dogs when I was small. The first reaction I experience when seeing a dog on the street is fear. Even though I have owned dogs and love them, my childhood trauma remains. The vagus nerve is essentially programmed by all inherited and personally obtained fear programs, although it can also help us clear them better than any other part of the nervous system.

You see, once your sympathetic nervous system gets alerted, it only takes seconds to amp into high gear. You could attempt to focus on boosting the calming hormones of your parasympathetic nervous system, but that will take ten to twenty minutes.[6] You

---

6. Dee Wagner, "Polyvagal theory in practice." *Counseling Today,* June 27, 2016. https://ct.counseling.org/2016/06/polyvagal-theory-practice/.

might even do a deep dive into healing the trauma's pain and suffering, but that usually takes years.

The best go-to is the vagus nerve, which we now understand as key to releasing acute or chronic stress because of a relatively new branch of science based on the polyvagal theory. This theory has emerged as consequential thanks to the work of Stephen W. Porges, a psychologist and research scientist.[7]

One unique part of the vagus nerve, which polyvagal theorists point out, is the dorsal vagal nerve, which relates to the parasympathetic system. When activated, that aspect of the vagus nerve can shut down our sympathetic panic reactions within milliseconds. Yet another stretch of the vagal nerve, called the ventral vagal nerve, can just as quickly restore us to a state of peace.[8]

Obviously, interacting with your vagus nerve is much more productive than over-mentalizing. It's also a quicker way to regain balance than many other therapeutic methods or medicines, although there is a place for all healing remedies. An even better piece of news is this: There are two extraordinary ways to activate and soothe your vagus nerve under stress, because everything is made of two types of energy.

What Does Energy Have to Do with Your Vagus Nerve?

So far, I've been describing your vagus nerve through only one lens: biology, which pertains to physical energy. As I shared in the introduction of this chapter, however, there are two types of energy. To empower your ability to perform calming maneuvers

7. Stephen W. Porges, PhD, "Polyvagal Theory," (website). https://www.stephenporges.com/.

8. Dee Wagner, "Polyvagal theory in practice," *Counseling Today*, June 27, 2016. https://ct.counseling.org/2016/06/polyvagal-theory-practice/.

on your vagus nerve, and even shift ingrained patterns of stress and trauma, it's vital to comprehend energy and both of its subdivisions. As background, everything is made of energy. That includes what you can and cannot see. Defined further, energy is simply information that vibrates.

Information is nothing more than influential data. There is information in a cup of coffee that tells it to be coffee. Guess what? If you alter that data, which is made of a complicated mess of molecules, atoms, and even subatomic or teeny-tiny particles, you could possibly transform your java into a cup of tea.

The other part of the quotient is vibration, or movement. We know that absolutely everything is in constant motion. You can't tell by peering into your coffee cup, but it's true. If you alter vibration, you change what is occurring with a substance (or anything else for that matter) from your mood to your motivation. Quicken the vibration of the liquid in a cappuccino and it will be steaming hot. And if you slow down those vibrations… let's put it this way: Do you really want to drink lukewarm coffee?

We're all well acquainted with physical energy, which is measurable. You can easily see, touch, taste, hear, or smell physical energy. Because the physical is so tangible, it's easy to understand how the autonomic nervous system reacts to physical stimuli.

For instance, when you spot a car running a stop sign, your system immediately ramps up. It can *see* that car. You can totally imagine getting hit! On go those sympathetic hormones, and everything else follows. Hopefully, your vagus nerve modulates your response and you slam on the brakes in time to avoid an accident.

Want another example? You hear a bump in the middle of the night. If you don't know what's causing it, you'll immediately become scared. Cranked into high gear, your autonomic system could convince you to hide under the covers, grab a baseball bat and scream, or slip out a nearby window.

While it's certainly valid to react to physical threats, most of what really endangers us is subtle. That's because 99.999-plus percent of all reality is composed of subtle rather than physical energy.[9] Subtle energies include those long-held and inaccurate fear patterns and programs, as well as what might occur in the invisible reality around us. I'll give you two examples.

Years ago, my youngest son had a newspaper delivery route. I don't know if you delivered newspapers when you were a kid or have helped a child do the same, but if you haven't, take my word for it: it's an excruciating process. Tops, my son made nine dollars a week for an eight-hour job: four hours of his time and four of mine.

On one particularly hot summer day, we were on opposite sides of a street. Each of us clutched a leash that was attached to a dog, and we each hauled a sack of rolled up papers on our backs. When we were ready to cross the street, I heard a voice yell in my head, "Tell him to STOP!" I didn't question the voice, which was inaudible to anyone but me. I yelled, "Stop!"

Gabe froze in his tracks. That was a good thing because a car barreled around the corner from another road. If Gabe hadn't ceased in his tracks, he would have been struck. Gabe's vagus nerve, in millisecond speediness, saved his life. The reason I knew that there was danger, however, wasn't due to everyday reality. Subtle energy packaged through my intuition saved the day—and his life.

As this story shows, subtle energy isn't bound by time. The message I received on that hot summer day from an invisible

9. Ali Sundermier, "99.9999999% of Your Body is Empty Space." *Science Alert*, September 23, 2016. https://www.sciencealert.com/99-9999999-of-your-body-is -empty-space.

source was predictive of the future. Subtle communiqués can also make their way from the past and other spaces into the present, in addition to being conveyed from possible futures. How do we scan for subtle energies? We use our intuition, or ability to receive, interpret, and send information psychically.

I'm going to share yet another example of how our autonomic nervous system, modulated by our speedy vagus nerve, can interact with subtle energy. We usually interpret those bumps in the middle of the night as physically induced, such as produced by a cat knocking over a lamp as opposed to a real thief trying to break in. Then again, those sounds might also be subtle in origin.

Years ago, after my son went off to college, I was awakened around midnight by the sound of footsteps. At that time, I slept downstairs with my two dogs, Honey and Lucky. Gabe's room was upstairs. It was a common experience to hear his heavy feet go *bang, bang, bang* when he rose to get a snack. During the night in question, however, there was no Gabe upstairs. Yet the sounds exactly matched those he would make.

I awoke with a startle. The dogs did so simultaneously. From the floor, they stood up and gazed at me, and me at them. I said, "Seek!" That was our code word for "Go upstairs and see what's going on." Both lay back on the floor and peered at their paws. The message was obvious. There was no way they were going to play super dogs.

Sighing, my heartbeat amiss and feeling quite breathless, I set my phone to 911, ready to press "dial" if need be, and quietly made my way up the stairs. There was nothing and no one there. My autonomic nervous system had picked up on psychic phenomena, which sounded physical but wasn't. Most likely, my intuition had heard the echo of my son's many forays to the kitchen.

Our intuition is always geared to inform our autonomic nervous system of possible dangers, and as I've shared, trying to think your way through a fright is incredibly slow. Fortunately, we can apply intuition to matters of stress not only to inform ourselves about what might be happening but also to trigger our vagus nerve into quick quietude.

Your Basic Intuitive Styles

You are naturally intuitive. Intuition is the means through which you receive and steer subtle energies that more easily and quickly affect your vagus nerve than your thoughts and most actions. It's far easier to access your intuitive faculties if you know what they are, so I'll next outline the four main types of intuition.

Two of these types are empathic, which means they are body-based. The other two abilities are verbal and visual. As you would expect, verbal and visual intuition are self-explanatory. Most of us are comfortable with a certain style rather than another. But what if you let yourself be surprised? You might find that you interrelate with all these modalities, and you can customize them to specific circumstances.

In a nutshell, the array of intuitive capabilities is as follow.

Physical Intuition

Physical intuitives receive guidance or messages or know what to do through bodily sensations. They sense what is happening within themselves, someone else, or the external world through taste, touch, smell, or another physical sensation. They might also be emotionally gifted and relate to others' feelings as if they are their own.

Then again, they might pick up on others' thoughts or beliefs, also getting data for the self through a sort of "gut knowing." Some physical empaths know what is occurring in nature and with natural beings, like animals or plants. And a few can direct natural and supernatural forces. Indigenous shamans do this when changing the weather or restoring calm to the seas.

Spiritual Intuition

Spiritual intuitives comprehend subtle energy through spiritual knowing. This capacity includes establishing through a oneness with Spirit (by whatever name is used) and operating from that knowing. The main difference between physical and spiritual intuitives is that people who are physically oriented gain their intuitive insights through their five senses, while spiritual intuitives sense information that emanates from higher sources of consciousness.

Verbal Intuition

The verbally gifted hears words, tones, or psychic guidance either inside their head or from outside it. They might also write, sing, or use some other auditory or musical medium to receive or share intuitive information, like through a song on the radio or words spoken by a character on television. In the psychic world, verbal intuition is also called clairaudience, which stands for "clear hearing."

Visual Intuition

The visual intuitive receives and sends psychic images. These are packaged in visions or pictures that might appear as colors, shapes, or even video shows. They can come through nightly dreams or daydreams, and maybe even via the environment, such as on a billboard. This capability is often called clairvoyance, which means "clear seeing."

You'll be employing your intuition in several of the exercises that are offered in the next part of this chapter, as we put all your vagus nerve knowledge to work.

The following exercises and suggestion can be used to activate your vagus nerve for health and wellbeing, both instantaneously and when dealing with deeper concerns.

Exercise
Spirit-to-Spirit

This exercise has several purposes. First, it can help you instantly activate the comforting abilities of your vagus nerve, no matter where you are or what's occurring. Second, it is a preparatory practice of many of the other techniques you'll learn in this chapter. With that in mind, I'll reference the steps of this exercise where I'd recommend you use it.

Basically, Spirit-to-Spirit is a process for safely accessing psychic information as well as performing healing, manifesting, prayer, meditation, and more. It creates boundaries to ensure only the highest outcome for everyone involved, no matter the request.

There are only three steps in this practice. As you walk through these steps, I'll explain what "spirit" means in each step. I'll also assist you with encouraging an immediate state of relaxation through an awareness of a stressor and your vagus nerve.

Step One: Affirm Your Personal Spirit. In this step, "spirit" refers to your unique spark of divinity. In this step, invoking your personal spirit equates with putting your highest self in charge.

As you recognize your personal spirit, focus on a stressor. Now request that this flame of divinity inside of you energetically link with your vagus nerve. This allows your spirit to begin to immediately alleviate that stress.

Step Two: Affirm Other Spirits. In this step, "spirit" has two meanings: it refers to the divinity within one or more living beings (even those involved in a stressor), as well as to the same in otherworldly beings.

We all have spiritual guides, which can include angels, the deceased, power animals, and the souls of plants or fairy beings, among others. When you acknowledge these spirits, you affirm that only the most loving can engage with your process.

Your personal spirit is now only going to interact with the highest aspects of all individuals involved in a stressor. You are also calling to you the presence of spiritual allies to provide support and assistance.

Step Three: Affirm the Spirit. In this process, the word "spirit" represents God, the Holy Spirit, Allah, the Greater Spirit, the Goddess, the Divine, the Greater Goodness, or whatever term you might use for your Higher Power. This is the most vital of all three steps. It basically invites a surrendering that will bring about the optimal outcome.

Allow yourself to sense the presence of the Spirit, the Divine, a goodness made of love. The Spirit can now work through your own divine spark, and the divinity of guidance and others involved with your stressor, to provide healing and soothing to your vagus nerve. You can now achieve restoration and rejuvenation.

Exercise
Practicing Your Intuition for Peace

While conducting this exercise, you'll be inadvertently alleviating stress while interacting intuitively. In fact, you'll be employing the four styles of intuition to imagine yourself from a ruffled into an unruffled state. Simply settle into a quiet space and follow these steps, beginning with Spirit-to-Spirit.

Step One: Affirm Your Personal Spirit. Go ahead! Invoke that inner flame of grace.

Step Two: Affirm Others' Spirits. You're connected to other living beings and spiritual allies. Know that for the duration of this exercise, you'll only be interconnecting with their highest energies.

Step Three: Surrender to the Spirit. Set the intention that the Spirit will now manage all aspects of the following steps. Settle into the knowledge that you are fully held, protected, and beloved by that divine force.

Step Four: Focus on a Stressor. Allow guidance to help you select a stressor. It might be physical, emotional, mental, or even spiritual. Once you're clear about this focus, move on to the next step.

Step Five: Employ Your Physical Intuition. Physically relate to the stressor. What does this tension or trauma feel like in your body, and where is it? What are the tastes, sensations, emotions, smells, or other factors composing this stress? Request that the Spirit clears this stressor out of your body tissues and leave peace in its place.

Step Six: Interact with Your Spiritual Intuition. Relate to the Spirit and guidance. What awareness do you receive from these loving sources about your stressor? When ready, rely on your bond with the Spirit and helpful spirits and allow them to insert serenity where there was strain.

Step Seven: Reveal the Verbal. Clear your mind and re-establish your bond with your own spirit, your spiritual guides, and the Spirit. Then request clairaudient messages related to your stressor.

What do you hear? What tones or other verbal messages do you become aware of, either in your mind or through the environment? When ready, ask for the words, song, sound, or other verbal communiqué that will alleviate the stress and restore stillness.

Step Eight: View the Visual. Breathe deeply into your diaphragm and bid that guidance provide a picture or set of images about the stress. Then ask that a healing image that holds the energies needed to achieve serenity replace the worrisome ones.

Step Nine: Let Peace Reign. All ways of knowing have assisted you in letting go of a stress and establishing a sense of peace. Feel the resulting joy.

Following are quick and easy exercises that are subdivided into two groups. The first list presents physical energetic tips and the second serves up subtle energetic tips for vagus nerve calming.

Shift Your Vagus Nerve Physically

Want some easy-to-use energy tips for vagus activation? Go for change in milliseconds with these physical energy tips. Try them all and mix and match as desired.

1. Get Chilled. One of the easiest ways to trigger your vagus nerve into a sudden state of relaxation is to expose yourself

to cold, like 50 degrees Fahrenheit or a bit colder.[10] If you're in winter weather, simply step outside for a few minutes (obviously, don't stay out there too long!). Do like the Finns and enjoy a sauna followed by a chilly jump in an icy lake, or just take a cold shower for a few minutes.

2. Sing, Sing, and Sing Some More. Singing and chanting stimulate the vagus nerve, sending waves of relaxation throughout you.[11] Belt out that rousing tune, either alone or with others, to tone up your vagus nerve. Even humming works!

3. Make Time for Massage. It turns out that massage stimulates the vagus nerve, especially if you work on specific areas of the body. Reflexology or foot massage especially decreases the fight and flight responses. If you can't get to a massage therapist, get a loved one to work on you.[12]

4. Roll Your Head. Author and vagus nerve expert Stanley Rosenberg is keen on helping you help yourself. His "Basic Exercise" can be done alone.

   Simply lie down face-up, interlacing your hands behind your head. Let your head rest gently on your hands and then slowly rotate all the way to one side. Return to center, and then rotate to the other side. Next, let your hands hold your head in the center, with your eyes open, for a full minute. In the next stage, you're just going to move your eyes all the

---

10. Tiina M. Makinen et al., "Autonomic nervous function during whole-body cold exposure before and after cold acclimation," *Aviation Space and Environmental Medicine*, September 2008, https://pubmed.ncbi.nlm.nih.gov/18785356/.

11. Yana Hoffman, RP, CCDC, and Hank Davis, PhD, "Sing in the Shower to Make Friends with Your Vagus Nerve." *Psychology Today*, March 17, 2020. https://www.psychologytoday.com/us/blog/try-see-it-my-way/202003/sing-in-the-shower-make-friends-your-vagus-nerve.

12. Ibid.

way to one side. Stay there for 30 to 60 seconds, then let your eyes travel back to the center. Rest for 30 to 60 seconds and repeat this action on the other side. Your eyes will tell you when to return to center, as you'll experience a sigh, yawn, or swallow.[13]

Shift Your Vagus Nerve Subtly

Let's awaken that vagus nerve for instant ease with these subtle energy practices.

1. Converse Until You're Converted. Talking with a loved one or friend is a sure way to break the spell of stress, as positive social bonding is known to improve vagal functioning.[14] What about if there isn't someone around to commune with? Maybe that person you most trust is part of your challenge?! So, employ your intuition to hold your own compassionate conversation. Conduct Spirit-to-Spirit, call upon a spiritual ally, and request that the spirit/s that show up provides you feelings, verbal messages, or images of love. Lean into the energetic presence of these beings, so all parts of you know you are held within community.

2. Stop Stress in Its Tracks. Spirit-to-Spirit can be undertaken in an instant to cease stress, but you might want to add another for-sure method. The tone "om" has been known amongst many spiritual cultures to achieve a higher state of consciousness called *samadhi*. In the West, we call it "flow."

---

13. Stanley Rosenberg, *Accessing the Healing Power of the Vagus Nerve* (Berkeley, CA: North Atlantic Books, 2017), 186–190.

14. Bethany E. Kok et al., "How positive emotions build physical health." *Psychological Science*, May 6, 2013. https://pubmed.ncbi.nlm.nih.gov/23649562/.

When under pressure, quickly walk through Spirit-to-Spirit while chanting Om internally or externally. You'll sense all-things spirit providing relief.

3. Breathe into Your Being. Your head and neck have receptors called "baroreceptors." When activated, they can awaken your vagus nerve and create ease in your system. One study shows that a slow yogic breathing called *ujjayi* is especially helpful for increasing the sensitivity and effectiveness of these baroreceptors.[15] By adding Spirit-to-Spirit and calling on guidance, you soothe the subtle energies underlying your stress. Simply conduct Spirit-to-Spirit and for a few minutes, breathe in five seconds per inhale and five seconds per exhale. Make sure these are belly breaths and let your own spirit fill in any empty gaps left by the releasing of stress energies.

4. Release the Deeper Trauma. As discussed earlier, the most challenging stressors can get stuck in the body to cause lodged trauma. Let your own spirit and guidance help you let go of old pain by first running through the above exercise, "Breathe into Your Being." While conducting your slow breathing, request that guidance show you a color representing the cause of the long-held stress. Then ask to perceive a healing color, one that can replace the hue associated with the causal issue. As these colors are swapped, slowly cease the ujjayi breathing and then, if you can, go enjoy the great

---

15. Joe Cohen, "19 Factors That May Stimulate Your Vagus Nerve Naturally." SelfDecode, November 3, 2021. https://health.selfdecode.com/blog/32-ways-to-stimulate-your-vagus-nerve-and-all-you-need-to-know-about-it/.

outdoors. Nature is especially replenishing for the vagus nerve and your autonomic nervous system.

It's a guarantee that life will arrange stressors on your path. But now, you can also meet yourself on the road of destiny, ready for all the delights of this world.

CHAPTER 8
Meditation Simplified
Shai Tubali

For a modern explorer, the booming meditation market can be both fascinating and overwhelming. Ancient meditation techniques are being rediscovered and adapted for twenty-first-century learners while new practices are constantly developed by meditation teachers. This vast array of techniques can lead you to a myriad of wondrous inner experiences. Furthermore, each of these practices offers unique keys to the art of meditation. Still, we need to be careful not to get lost in this abundance. Meditation itself should be kept simple. In fact, you can learn how to meditate even without delving into any of these techniques.

Meditation, after all, is not a technique but a certain quality or approach of your mind. While there are numerous meditative practices, there is only one meditative approach. When you become familiar with this approach, you can invoke meditative calm at any given moment, wherever you are. The only tool that you require is your own mind. To return to these basics of meditation, let us start our journey by learning about Tilopa's six words of advice.

Don't Meditate

Tilopa was a highly influential Buddhist master who lived in India between the years 988 and 1069. His six well-known instructions on what to do in meditation are an excerpt from a spiritual song called the "Doha Treasure" that Tilopa sang to his student Naropa. These concise instructions are perfect for helping us to be in an authentically meditative state.

Here are Tilopa's six words of advice, in Ken McLeod's translation:[1]

Don't recall. Let go of what has passed.

Don't imagine. Let go of what may come.

Don't think. Let go of what is happening now.

Don't examine. Don't try to figure anything out.

Don't control. Don't try to make anything happen.

Rest. Relax, right now, and rest.

The first thing we read about the meditative approach is that it involves letting go of the past. Recalling your past can sometimes be meaningful. For instance, therapeutic processes encourage you to revisit past events so that you can come to terms with them and release their burdens. You may also wish to cherish some of the remarkable experiences that inspire you to this day. But from a meditative point of view, the past has already passed. How could busying yourself with what has passed lead you to meditative calm? The fragrance of meditation is therefore past-free.

In any case, the past now exists only as a picture inside your mind. To even know the past, you need to conjure up a picture in your mind. Right now, do you have any evidence to show that you have a past? Of course not. Such evidence requires the existence of

---

1. Repa Dorje Odzer, "Tilopa's Six Nails."

an image or picture. But this evidence is just thought. Right now, your reality doesn't have a past.

Then Tilopa points out that meditation also involves letting go of the future. He refers to our thoughts about the future as "imagining." This is because the future, like the past, exists only in pictures: our pictures of tomorrow, or of ten years from now. These pictures are sometimes worrisome and sometimes motivating. In general, they constitute a healthy part of our functioning. It is good to plan ahead and to try to predict certain events with either anticipation or caution. These predictions, Tilopa remarks, may or may not come true. But when it comes to meditative calm, meditation is not the time to let your imagination run wild. There will be plenty of time to do that later. Now it is time to be future-free.

If you can be without a sense of past or future for even one long moment, you are already steeped in meditation. I will explain later what you should do if thoughts about the past or the future appear to draw your attention during meditation. But if you can see that neither past or future exist right now—or exist only as pictures in your mind—you may realize that letting go of them for a while is a real possibility.

At this point, you might think, "Okay, I'm willing to let go of what has passed and what may come, but at least I have the present." No. Tilopa is taking away your present too, because he says, "Don't think. Let go of what is happening now." Naturally, when you're busy responding to challenging situations or fulfilling mundane tasks, you cannot avoid considering what is happening. But why would you carry your roles and duties into your meditative calm? In meditation, you have no role to play. You are not needed. We tend to assume that we should carry the burden of the world on our shoulders all the time. For this reason, many of us often struggle to fall asleep: even when we don't have to, we try to control what is happening. Meditation is the permission that you give yourself to cease functioning as the world's manager, at least for a little while.

Tilopa's first three tips are all about time: letting go of thoughts that have anything to do with the past, present, and future. There is no need to keep your mind tethered to the movement of time. Meditation, Tilopa tells us, is immersing oneself in a state of timelessness.

But Tilopa has more to say about the meditative approach. First, he advises us to avoid examining and trying to figure things out. Remember, this is not advice for a good life. Most of the time, we do need to make sense of what is happening in our life. But meditation is not the time to look into anything. Khenchen Thrangu Rinpoche translates Tilopa's advice a little differently, as "don't meditate on anything."[2] This may sound perplexing: how can Tilopa recommend that in our meditation, we avoid meditating? The original Latin meaning of meditation describes a state of intense contemplation, of "thinking deeply about something."[3] This may imply that the practice of meditation is always a meditation on a specific object. Indeed, many meditation techniques seek to focus your attention on one thing, such as a mantra (a sacred word or sound) or your breathing process. This focal point can help you dissolve the familiar state of a scattered mind and harness the power of your attention.

However, think for a moment of how it feels when you enter meditation with the determination to meditate on something and to work at it. Tilopa is clearly aware of this self-defeating approach.

2. Thrangu, *Tilopa's Wisdom*, 157.

3. Lexico, s.v. "Meditate," accessed August 10, 2022, https://www.lexico.com/definition/meditate.

He insists that the actual practice of meditation consists in *not* trying to do anything. Meditative calm invites you to leave the habit of doing and making effort behind. It offers you instead the opportunity to revel in a state of relaxed openness.

Tilopa's fifth piece of advice on meditation is to avoid controlling the practice and trying to make something happen. Normally, it is reasonable to try to control our actions and to direct events in our life so that they lead to welcome outcomes—at least as long as we accept that much of what is happening cannot be fully controlled. Moreover, you take certain actions because you hope to achieve specific results. But when you enter meditation with a determined purpose, you inevitably become obsessed with your wish to experience exactly what you have in mind. Instead of relaxed openness, you find yourself continuously analyzing your meditation session and making sure that your practice is just like this or that: "Am I going in the right direction? Am I missing something? Do I understand it correctly?" Thus in his fourth and fifth instructions, Tilopa shows us that meditation is not a focused activity that is done with the intention of gaining something else as a result. When you act rather than meditate, your mind becomes so concentrated that it is like a fist instead of the open hand it is meant to be. Can you imagine realizing anything when your mind is like a fist?

The receptive state of the open hand is what meditation feels like. If you stop recalling, imagining, thinking, examining, and controlling, your mind becomes completely loose and sinks into meditative calm. Notice that Tilopa's first five words of advice are not formulated as things that you should do or focus on, but as things that you should cease to do. When we express the wish to learn to meditate, we usually seek out clear guidelines on how to practice. Tilopa, on the other hand, emphasizes that the essence of meditation lies not in what you do but in what you don't. For this reason, he sometimes refers to his vision of meditation as the "state of nonmeditation."[4]

Tilopa's last piece of advice is not only an additional guideline but also the natural state that remains after you've followed these five forms of letting go. Try to communicate with this for a moment: what would happen if you put aside what has passed, what may come, and what is happening now, and also ceased to figure anything out and to make anything happen? The final outcome is Tilopa's last advice: "Rest." In other words, meditation is simply a state of deep restfulness.

Tilopa's intention behind the word "rest" is profound. He speaks of a deep loosening of the clinging of the mind—releasing your grip and being here, right now, with the mind completely open. Try to feel how burdened a mind can be when it is doing all these activities. It is a mind that clings all day long to what has passed, what may come, what is happening now, figuring something out, and making something happen. The unfortunate reality is that this is most people's persistent state of mind. Approaching your meditation as if it were one more thing to do is thus counterproductive. But if you let yourself rest in meditation, the difference between doing and just being will finally become clearer.

This is the foundation: meditation is actually nonmeditation. Now let's explore four key principles that will allow us to truly abide in meditative rest.

First Principle: Set Your Intention

Even if we long for the state of meditative calm, the lifelong habit of recalling, imagining, thinking, examining, and controlling often

---

4. Nyenpa, *Tilopa's Mahamudra Upadesha*, 11.

overpowers our good intentions. We have simply become used to contemplating these issues all the time. One of the best ways to prevent this habit from interfering with our nonmeditation is setting an intention just before the practice. A conscious intention can diminish your tendency to produce and hold on to thoughts of this type.

Modern meditations hardly ever use the power of intention. We go into the practice and hope for the best. Sometimes we have a "good" meditation, but too often we spend this precious time being aimlessly distracted. On the other hand, many forms of traditional practice acknowledge the need for this type of preparation. In Buddhism, for instance, meditators often enter into meditation with the declared intention to benefit all sentient beings. In this way, they cultivate *bodhicitta*, an awakened mind.[5]

A declared intention can give direction to your practice. As soon as you clarify your intent, all your internal forces are gathered into one flow of attention. But don't confuse intention with a goal-oriented spirit. Bringing a goal-oriented spirit into your practice would imply that you have every intention of remaining busy and focused—in other words, *doing* meditation. The intention that you express, however, is all about ceasing to try to figure everything out and to make something happen. You declare that you are willing to leave the world behind for a short while and that you are therefore temporarily more interested in being than in doing. This gives a signal to your mind to become aligned with this mode of being.

As soon as you declare why you are going to meditate, you bring totality into the practice. The entire practice becomes instantly colored with your intention. Do not think of your intention as a form of prayer. It is not like saying, "Please, God, make it

---

5. Drolma, "How to Practice Dedicating Merit."

a good meditation!" Setting an intention is not about hoping that the meditation will be good. Intention is not powerless—rather it is one of the most powerful things in life.

In general, your meditation could be directed to advancing world peace, or to emanating beauty and purity in the world. You could even meditate with the purpose of enhancing your relationships. But if you wish to tap into the meditative calm that Tilopa offers, the most accurate choice would be to clarify that you intend to abandon your usual focus and the tendency to examine and control. Since you are confident that the world and the endless stream of time can wait for you until you have completed your sitting, you are resolute in your wish to take an internal holiday. All the problems you are expected to resolve and all the big or small decisions you are supposed to make can be momentarily withheld. You are not going to waste your meditation on continuing to do what you already do all day long.

Your intention could follow this approach: "In entering this meditation, I'm leaving the world behind. I don't care what's going to happen. Right now I'm not going to solve any problems. It's none of my business. I'm not interested in looking back on memories and regrets, nor am I interested in making future plans. This is the time for deep restfulness. I just am, without focus or aim." As soon as you utter these simple words and close your eyes, you will notice that suddenly, the meditation is far more awake and energetic.

Second Principle:
Understand the Law of Attention

You are sitting for meditation. After clarifying your conscious intention to leave the world behind, you are beginning to ease yourself into a state of natural restfulness. For several long, happy moments, your mind is aligned with your intention. But then, the all-too-familiar stream of thoughts resumes, and you feel that your restless mind won't allow you to meditate. You may even feel as if you are under attack, as if you are now a victim of your own mind. From this point on, your meditation becomes a wearisome struggle: ironically, you are fighting your way back to inner peace.

After several frustrating experiences, some aspiring medita- tors begin to refer to their mind as if it were a mere interference or even an enemy. The mind becomes synonymous with inner chaos and conflict. But your mind is neither an interference nor an enemy. In fact, when you understand the second principle, you can easily bring your mind back to its natural, luminous state.

Meditation is the mind's ability to put itself back into order. Your wonderful, lucid mind has simply become intermixed with certain thoughts and emotions, but it has the power to choose to stop being so. The Law of Attention shows you how your mind can give rise to stress and struggle, but also how it can do the very opposite and bring itself to a state of meditative calm. This can be achieved by making use of a certain power that you have always possessed but whose significance you have rarely acknowledged: your attention.

Attention is the act of directing your mind to listen, see, or understand. But just before you direct your mind toward some- thing, you *choose* to do so, because you believe that paying atten- tion to it would be meaningful, relevant, or rewarding to you. This means that there is a gap between you and every thought that you ever have. In this gap, you have the power to choose to give atten- tion to the thought or not.

Think of it this way: before your attention and your thoughts became inseparably intermixed, there was awareness and choice. The fact that a certain thought passes through your mind and your attention becomes so automatically entangled with it is because you are no longer aware of the gap and the choice. In meditation, you can finally recover the power of your attention that has been lost in the endless stream of thoughts.

This is what your meditative practice begins to teach you: that you can easily separate attention from thinking. Mostly, we are unaware of this distinction. Our attention is glued to our thinking as if it were one process. But in the gap between attention and thinking, our entire freedom lies.

According to the Law of Attention, the very nature of attention is to act as the light that shines on something. When your attention shines on a certain thought, this thought instantly becomes your reality. Then you begin to feel—physically, mentally, and emotionally—according to the reality you created through your attention. Attention is like the food that thoughts require: in the same way that your body needs food and water, thoughts feed on your attention. On the other hand, that which you do not give attention to becomes completely powerless and meaningless.

It is up to you alone: *you* give the power to thoughts. This implies that there are no powerful thoughts. No one in the world can claim that a certain thought is too powerful and too overwhelming to handle. Thoughts cannot take over you unless you let them do so. All your habitual thoughts are just things that *you* have decided to attach your attention to.

Your practice becomes taxing only when you are not aware of the Law of Attention and are wasting your precious time on trying to control or push away these thoughts. Any attempt to control these elements will only get you caught up in another conflict; you cannot, in fact, control them. The only thing you can control is your attention, which means owning your own mind.

Meditation is the discovery of the power of your attention and your capacity to free it from any kind of dependency on thoughts. So, when you detect a thought, start experiencing the gap between it and attention, and allow yourself to rest in it for a while. While you are absorbed in meditation, you don't have to give the power of attention to any of your thoughts. In life, you naturally have to choose certain thoughts and emotions to identify with. When you make a decision, you pick one of the options that your thinking has offered you. But what reason would you have to focus on a particular thought while meditating? After all, there is nothing you are supposed to do or achieve.

During practice, keep your attention unfocused. Unfocused means pure attention. It means that you are fully attentive, but not attentive toward anything in particular. You don't waste your energy. In this way, your mind returns to its original state of meditative calm.

When Tilopa advises us to stop recalling, imagining, thinking, examining, and controlling, he doesn't mean that we should busy ourselves with pushing away thoughts about past events, future plans, or present challenges. Remember, this can only end in inner struggle. What Tilopa really means is that you should stop giving attention to all these thoughts. There is absolutely no need to exercise your power of attention. Instead, you choose to rest.

Third Principle: Don't Silence Your Mind

When we think of meditative calm, we tend to imagine a state in which there is not a single thought interfering with our inner quietude. As a result, meditators often sit for meditation in anticipation of this extraordinary state. They suppose that as long as the current of thoughts persists, meditation is not possible. But this would mean that your meditative calm is forever dependent on the unpredictable fluctuation of your thoughts.

Naturally, sitting and waiting for something to happen cannot lead to restfulness, but only to tension. If you are continuously thinking, "I need to be in a state of peace. I need to have a silent mind," you are trying to fabricate an unusual state—in other words, you are caught up in "examining" and "controlling." Even if this state did appear in your meditation, you wouldn't be able to grasp it. Sooner or later, this state would have to disappear, and the more familiar condition of a mind enwrapped in thoughts would reappear.

It can be inspiring to read about some extraordinary mystics, such as the twentieth-century philosopher Jiddu Krishnamurti, who have claimed to have no thoughts for hours on end.[6] But it can also be frustrating and confusing. Must you reach this unusual state to be able to enjoy meditative calm? Fortunately, the calm for which we aim in meditation is of a different type. In reality, you don't need to quiet your thoughts down to settle into a state of profound calmness. A fulfilling meditation has nothing to do with how boisterous or relaxed your thoughts are.

Remember, the peace of mind lies in the effortlessness of meditation. This effortlessness also applies to the way you relate to your thoughts. You already know, based on the Law of Attention, that you don't have to enhance any of your thoughts through the power of attention. You simply rest in the gap between you and your thoughts. This also means that you don't have to make the effort of reacting to any of them. You can just let them be—and when you let your thoughts be, you finally let yourself be.

---

6. Krishnamurti, *Total Freedom*, 153, 155.

A noisy mind is like birds chirping on a tree nearby. Unless you are unusually sensitive, it is difficult to imagine that you would be disturbed by your neighborhood's chatty birds. In fact, you have probably gotten used to this background stream of noise to a degree that you are mostly unaware of its existence. Understandably, you are too engrossed in your own world to notice. In the very same way, you can be engrossed in your meditative calm while thoughts pass through your mind. Only if you believe that these mental chirps are significant—only if you choose to give them the power of attention—can these bubbles of thought appear to rob you of your inner quietude.

Struggling to quiet your mind is as futile as hushing the house sparrows in a nearby tree would be. Neither will listen to you. Fight your mind, and you will end up experiencing a split within yourself. Suddenly you are two: the silencer and the naughty thoughts you observe. This doesn't make sense. But you will only get caught in this hopeless battle if you believe that the calm you are looking for is one that cannot tolerate or contain the presence of thoughts.

Meditative calm is not the opposite of thoughts. It can accommodate all thoughts in the same way that the cosmic space contains the luminous stars. This is the discovery of your inner space. You don't tap into this space when all thoughts are gone. You find it at the background in all your thoughts, or just beneath them, or, as instructed in the Buddhist Dzogchen meditation, in the spaces between one thought and another.[7] This is probably the most liberating point: in the effortless peace of nonmeditation, there can be no interference. Nothing can challenge this peace, since everything is welcomed and included in it.

---

7. Berzin, "Steps of Dzogchen Meditation."

You realize how beautiful meditation can be only when meditation is no longer about bringing yourself to a certain condition. Instead, you find peace of mind by not attempting to change anything. You are attentive and aware, free from the need to act or react. You are equally observing all changing states: sometimes your thoughts are talkative, and at other moments, your mind is silent. But you have no preference for one state or another. You are not especially exhilarated when your mind happens to be silent. You are not irritated when a ripple of thought seems to disturb the stillness of your inner pond. In both conditions, you just "relax, right now, and rest."

Fourth Principle: Meditation Is Your Natural State

There is one final, delicate point. It is about how we read and respond to Tilopa's sixth word of advice:

Rest. Relax, right now, and rest.

When someone advises you to rest and relax, how do you follow this advice? Even sinking into a state of restfulness may sound like an effortful action: currently I am under a lot of stress, but I'd like to move to a relaxed mode of being. There is still a sense of distance, like moving from X to Y. We can imagine it as taking a walk inside ourselves and finally coming to a certain realm. But Tilopa wants us to relax "right now," not a moment later. How can this relaxation happen in a flash?

Thrangu Rinpoche translates Tilopa's sixth piece of advice as "Just rest naturally."[8] "Naturally" is the key: It indicates that the restfulness of meditation is your natural state. Your current stressful condition may be more familiar to you, but it is not your

---

8. Thrangu, *Tilopa's Wisdom*, 157.

natural state. On the other hand, this state of restfulness already exists within you, even if you have never been aware of its presence. There is no point in striving to create or achieve meditative calm: all you have to do is reveal it and relax into it. More than that, because meditative calm is already there, hidden inside you, any effortful action you make can only lead you away from it.

In Mahayana Buddhism, this natural state is referred to as your "Buddha-nature."[9] In Vajrayana Buddhism, it is believed that each of us possesses a "very subtle mind," which is an already perfectly meditative layer of the mind.[10] This underlying reality within you is the reason that you don't need to try to make anything happen. Instead, you find this restful state beneath your thoughts, or in the spaces between one thought and another. It is always available to you. Meditation is simply the time in which you grow aware of your mind's true nature.

This is a very subtle secret: beneath the superficial layers of your thoughts, your mind is already calm. In fact, as Tilopa himself says elsewhere, your mind is like space.[11] Since you constantly pay attention to certain thoughts within your mind, you hardly ever notice the space in which these thoughts are contained. But thoughts appear and fluctuate within a certain space. Your attention tends to focus on what stands out in space, in the same way that you mainly notice stars when you look up at the night sky. On the other hand, when you look into the space of your mind, you realize that the thoughts that have kept you so busy are a miniscule percentage of the vast space of your mind. The reason you can "rest naturally" is that your mind has significantly more space than thoughts.

---

9. *Tricycle*, "What is Buddhanature?"

10. Yeshe, *The Bliss of Inner Fire*, 87–88.

11. Nyenpa, *Tilopa's Mahamudra Upadesha*, 3.

So, when you meditate, you just need to tune in to the natural state of your mind. It is as simple as tuning a radio and switching the station just slightly. Think of it as a type of meditation that is already taking place—you just weren't participating in it. This calm cannot be lost. It doesn't depend on the absence of thinking, and the presence of thoughts cannot rob you of it. It is not a fabricated pause, a point of relaxation in the midst of your mental noise. It is a recognition of the fundamental calmness of your mind.

When Tilopa prescribes nonmeditation, it is because he doesn't want you to overlook this natural reality of your mind. For this reason, his first five words of advice are concerned only with what you should stop doing. His last piece of advice points at the restfulness that is uncovered as a result. Although Tilopa was a superb meditation teacher, who taught complex techniques of breathing and visualization, he wanted to make sure that his students would never forget this basic truth of meditation.

You cannot "do" meditation. "Doing" meditation is based on the belief that meditation is an act. In fact, the only thing in the world that you surely *cannot* do is meditation. It is just not possible, since meditation is by its nature nonaction, the moment when you cease to act. This also implies that even though you can study countless meditation techniques, you cannot learn meditation: meditation itself is the art of unlearning certain mental habits that keep you from experiencing meditative calm.

Even if you can only devote five minutes a day to not recalling, imagining, thinking, examining, or controlling, it should be enough to color your daily experience. The quality of these five minutes, during which you have left the world behind and bathed in your mind's natural restfulness, will imbue all your activities with meditative calm.

Bibliography

Berzin, Alexander. "Steps of Dzogchen Meditation." *Study Buddhism*. Accessed July 18, 2022. https://studybuddhism.com/en/advanced-studies/vajrayana/dzogchen-advanced/how-to-meditate-on-dzogchen/steps-of-dzogchen-meditation.

Drolma, Lama Palden. "How to Practice Dedicating Merit." *Lion's Roar*, March 10, 2022. https://www.lionsroar.com/how-to-practice-dedicating-merit/.

Krishnamurti, Jiddu. *Total Freedom*. New York: HarperCollins, 1996.

Nyenpa, Sangyes. *Tilopa's Mahamudra Upadesha*. Translated by David Molk. Boston: Snow Lion, 2014.

Odzer, Repa Dorje. "Tilopa's Six Nails" [online]. *Tricycle* (Spring 2018). Accessed July 19, 2022. https://tricycle.org/magazine/tilopas-six-nails/.

Thrangu, Khenchen. *Tilopa's Wisdom*. Boulder, CO: Snow Lion, 2019.

Tricycle. "What is Buddhanature?" Accessed July 19, 2022. https://tricycle.org/beginners/buddhism/what-is-buddhanature/.

Yeshe, Lama. *The Bliss of Inner Fire*. Somerville, MA: Wisdom, 1998.

CHAPTER 9

FIND CALM THROUGH EFT AND TAPPING

Amy B. Scher

Emotional Freedom Technique, often called EFT or tapping, came into my life when I needed it most, when I was working hard to heal from chronic illness and struggling with so much fear and anxiety. It's been over a decade since I've healed completely, in part thanks to this amazing technique. But even though I'm well now, I use it all the time, in many different ways, which I'll be sharing with you in this chapter.

What Exactly Is Emotional Freedom Technique (EFT)?

Emotional Freedom Technique is a technique that combines the principles of acupuncture (minus the needles) and talking about unresolved emotional issues in order to release them. It's a simple and effective tool based on the meridian system, a system of energy pathways in the body, originating in Chinese medicine thousands of years ago. EFT was developed in the early 1990s by Stanford graduate and engineer Gary Craig. Along the meridians are special points commonly used in acupuncture that can be utilized to move energy and remove blockages. Where there is an imbalance, there is a corresponding blockage in the meridian system that contributes to emotional and physical symptoms. Gently tapping with the fingertips works to release these blockages and restore balance.

By restoring balance to the body's energy system, we are bringing our body into a calmer state that results in less stress and more positive feelings such as calm, hope, and peace.

In simple terms, this is how I see it working: Imagine your dog, Rufus, totally freaks out every time the mailman comes to the door. Each day, you tell Rufus in your most calming voice that he's okay and safe around Mr. Mailman. Chances are Rufus will look at you like you don't know what you're talking about and continue to bark in fear. But if you kneel down next to him and pat him, calming him at the same time he is looking at the mailman *while* Rufus is being triggered by fear, you'll ultimately be changing the pattern of what happens to Rufus in his body when he sees the mailman. His system will reprogram itself to be okay and balanced in the mailman's presence. We're basically going to do the same thing for you. We're going to change what happens to you in your energy body when you are triggered by emotions that cause stress. Triggers can be anything: the news, difficult relationships, unresolved feelings from the past, and more.

EFT is one of the most diverse techniques I know. I'm going to be giving you some really simple applications for it in this chapter, and if you love them, I encourage you to learn how to use it even more ways to help you find peace and calm in your life.

The Tapping Points

Even if you're already familiar with Emotional Freedom Technique, follow along with me. I do it a bit differently than many practitioners, so you might just learn something new or fun. This technique has endless possibilities; while I cover the building blocks and some extra tips and tricks in this chapter, there is much more you can continue to learn.

The first thing you need to know to use EFT is where you will actually be tapping on your face and body. You don't need to do anything with this yet; I just want you to understand where to tap when we're ready.

Just know that, as much as you want to aim for the points I describe, it's okay if you're slightly off. The tapping creates a percussion effect that vibrates through the associated energy pathway, and does the job of clearing. Even kids learn this technique, so I promise it's very easy! Just take it one step at a time.

EFT Tapping Points

Karate chop point—The outside of your hand about halfway between the bottom of your pinky and your wrist. This is where you would break a board if you were a martial artist.

Top of the head—This is smack dab in the middle of the top of your head.

Eyebrow—The inside corner of your eye, right where your eye-brow starts.

Side of the eye—Outer corner of the eye, right on the bone. It's right inside your temple, closer to your eye.

Under the eye—Top of the cheekbone, right under your eye.

Under the nose—This is where a moustache would be if you had one.

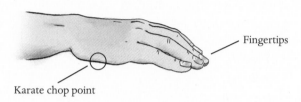

Fingertips

Karate chop point

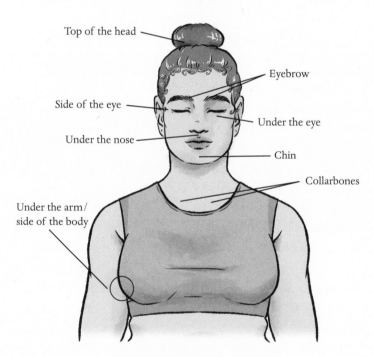

Top of the head

Eyebrow

Side of the eye

Under the eye

Under the nose

Chin

Collarbones

Under the arm /
side of the body

EFT tapping points

Chin—In the indentation on your chin, halfway between your bottom lip and the tip of your chin.

Collarbone—Find where a necktie would be tied, then go out to each side an inch and drop directly under the collarbone.

Under the arm/side of the body—This is where a bra band sits, about four inches under your armpit on the side of your body.

Fingertips—On each finger, tap in the lower right-hand corner of the fingernail, where the nail meets the cuticle. It's not necessary to be precise as long as you aim for the lower right-hand corner.

Tapping Point Tips

For the tapping points located on both sides of the body, you can tap on just one side of the body or on both sides. I am a lazy tapper and use only one side of the body. It works just the same, so feel free to do whatever is comfortable for you.

You want to tap about five to seven times in each spot (no need to count) using medium pressure. Feel it out. You can't mess up, so just relax and use this as a practice of undoing your perfection- ism. Just make sure you use your fingertips and not your nails. If the points are sore, it generally means the associated meridian is congested and needs to be cleared, so tap gently.

There are various shortcut forms of EFT out there, some of which skip tapping points to save time. I always use all the points, as each one corresponds with a different energy pathway and different organs, glands, muscles, and more. We want to make sure we cover all the bases and clear all the energy imbalances or blockages related to these feelings. It's not necessary to save ten seconds for a shortcut.

Tap to Find Calm

Now that you have the tapping points down, we're going to go to the next step. Just keep in mind that the ultimate goal of this technique is to vent about the emotions and feelings you are experiencing, and tap to neutralize or clear it in your energy system. That's it. Talk as if you were telling a friend about how you feel and tap. I usually talk out loud, but if you are unable to do this or are uncomfortable with it, you can talk in your head.

While using Emotional Freedom Technique, being as specific as you can in describing how you feel will help you get the best results.

We're going to do this by using a few easy steps:

Close your eyes and tune in to how you feel right now (rate the intensity from 1 to 10, 10 being most intense).

Create a set-up statement, which I'll show you how to do shortly.

Use your set-up statement while tapping the karate chop point.

Tap through the rest of the points.

Check-in and repeat

Wrap up

Step 1: Rate the Intensity of Your Feelings

On a scale of 1 to 10, rate how you feel right now in terms of *stress or anxiety* (this can include feelings of fear, anger, or any other emotions you may feel). A rating of 10 will be the strongest. If you can locate where you feel it in your body, also take note of that. Some examples: a burning in your chest, pit in your stomach, or fuzzy feeling in your head. Not everyone feels emotion in their body, so if you feel nothing, that's okay too.

It doesn't matter how intense your feelings are right now; it's just good to have an idea of your starting point so you can gauge your progress as you clear.

Step 2: Create a Set-Up Statement

We always start with what we call a *set-up statement*. Using this statement, we are setting up our tapping session by acknowledging the issue we're dealing with but are sending the message that we can let it go, move on, and feel calm.

Here is the entire statement:

"Even though I feel _____ (describe how you feel), I choose to let it go and feel calm."

First part of statement: "Even though I feel _____ (describe how you feel)..."

Use as much descriptive detail as possible to "call out" the energy of those feelings in your system so they can be cleared. You want to bring them up to acknowledge them so they can be processed and moved through your system. Your statement might look something like this:

"Even though I feel scared about _____ and I feel this pitter-patter in my heart when I think about it, ..."

> **Tip:** Try to mix a physical symptom and an emotional feeling into this statement. Think of using this set-up statement as a way to tell the body about the problem you wish to clear.

Second part of statement: "I choose to let it go and feel calm."

Here you will use this positive statement to balance the set-up statement. You are essentially telling yourself that even though you feel some negative feelings (first part), it is okay and you can feel calm (second part).

Once you have both parts of the statement ready, you can move on to the next step.

Step 3: Say Your Set-Up Statement While
Tapping the Karate Chop Point

To begin the EFT process, say the entire statement you put together three times in a row as you tap the karate chop point continuously. Use three or four fingers of one hand and tap the karate chop point of the other.

You can say the same exact statement three times, or you can vary the wording slightly. As long as whatever you are saying is true for you, it will work.

I always tap with my eyes closed so I can really focus on what's coming up instead of getting distracted by my environment.

Let's try it now with your eyes closed. Repeat your set-up statement three times. Here's an example:

"Even though I feel scared about _____ and I feel this pitter-patter in my heart when I think about it, I choose to let it go and feel calm."

Now you are ready to move on to the rest of the tapping points we talked about earlier.

Step 4: Tap through the Rest of the Points

Next, you are simply going to tap through the rest of the points while you vent more about how you feel. By venting, I mean you will pretend you're talking to a friend—just let loose! While you tap, talk and talk about whatever is bothering you. Try using a mix of emotional and physical sensations in your descriptions; that is, talk about how you feel emotionally and how it's making you feel physically.

This round of tapping might include statements such as:

"I just feel so _____"

"I can't stop thinking/worrying about _____"

"I have all these feelings of _____"

Continue with your own words. If you feel like you don't know what to say, again: just imagine talking to a friend about these feelings. It will really help you to say what's coming up without overthinking it.

Remember, you are just bringing up the yucky energy so it can move out. It may not feel great to temporarily focus on it, but it's the only way to really clear it deeply so you can get to a calmer, better place.

> **Tip:** You don't need to use complete sentences. You can use phrases, single words, or descriptions that only you understand. Aim to tap about 5 to 7 times at each point; or one phrase, sentence, or idea for each point. Just talk about whatever is true for you in this moment. It's your time to vent all those feelings from your body.

You want to continue through the points for a few rounds (karate chop to karate chop) or about 5 to 10 minutes before you take a break.

Step 5: Check In and Repeat

Take a break, open your eyes, take a deep breath or two, and check in with yourself. Give the energy a little bit of time to process and shift.

Now close your eyes and tune back in to your body. Rate the intensity of how you feel again on a scale of 1 to 10, 10 being the strongest. Notice if either the physical sensation or the emotional rating has gone down at all. Did it improve? If not, it's no biggie. Occasionally a person will shift with just a few minutes, but not everyone does. I am my own worst client, as it often takes me many rounds and then sometimes even lots of processing time after that to feel a shift in my system. If you aren't feeling any relief, you'll want to repeat the entire process again from the beginning, either with the same words or different words that ring true for you.

If you feel increased intensity after your first round, that's okay. Any change is actually a great sign that the imbalanced energy is mobilizing and transforming. People will often feel a temporary surge in emotion or symptoms as they tap. Again, this is simply because we are bringing things to the surface or stirring them up as part of the release process. They may have been buried deep and are rising close to the surface to be cleared. Hooray! This is exactly what we want.

Do you feel like you're starting to calm down or feel even slightly better about your situation? Sometimes while clearing, release of energy or improved balance will show up in the following ways: feeling more calm in your body, feeling more optimistic, suddenly seeing things in a way you didn't before, or feeling like you care less about whatever you were stressed or worried about before.

Now repeat the tapping and venting for a few more rounds. Take a few deep breaths and focus on the issue again. Rate it and decide if you should keep going. If not, you're ready to wrap up. Great job!

Step 6: Wrap Up

When you're feeling better or need to take a tapping break until another session, it's nice to wrap up with some positive tapping. It's important to only do this at the very end of your session. Tapping and saying positive things all day will not clear any negative feelings from your system. You need to address things in the way I've described in order to do that.

To close with a positive round, simply do one last tapping round focusing on some positive or calming phrases. Tap once through all the points using a phrase such as: *I can be calm now.*

That's it! You successfully used EFT.

How Long Should You Tap?

Many people make the mistake of tapping for only a couple minutes, only to say, "Tapping doesn't work." While tapping can feel like a miracle once you learn and use it successfully, it does often take more than a few minutes to get there. Gary Craig says that the three most important aspects of EFT are persistence, persistence, and persistence! You simply need to keep tapping and working through the process as many times as it takes. When the energy of the experience is truly cleared from your system, you will likely have a more distant or faded vision of your memory. It will feel like it happened to someone else or like it's just "there now" instead of holding a strong emotional charge like it did before.

EFT Reminders

Emotional Freedom Technique really is a wonderful technique that is easily adaptable. Here are some points to keep in mind as you practice using it:

Remember that you don't have to talk out loud when using EFT. Talking out loud is often helpful, but you can talk quietly in your head if necessary.

If tapping agitates you for any reason, use the alternate "touch and breathe" technique: touch one point and take a breath, then move on to the next point.

Remember that to clear energy, you must bring it up. Don't distract yourself from feeling discomfort during this process.

Don't jump into positive tapping until you're all finished. The positive round is used only when you're ready to wrap up your session so you can end on a positive note.

If you don't feel as though the old energy is clearing from your system, ask yourself this question about whatever issue you're working on: "Is there something under this issue bothering me?" For instance, if you're mad at your brother for saying something rude and tapping is not resulting in a shift, ask yourself if there's another aspect you could be missing. Are you upset at others for not defending you? Frustrated with yourself that you don't have better boundaries? Try tapping on those feelings too and it's likely you will see greater relief.

Ways to Use EFT

While Emotional Freedom Technique is exceptional, clients often get stuck on what to say while tapping and feel discouraged from using it. While the words you use are not nearly as important as you may think—because bringing up the feeling or emotion is how we actually get effective clearing—it is still a very real stumbling block for some. Here are some solutions for you to try.

Use It in the Moment

This is the way we've been practicing EFT so far together. But for really stressful times, I'm going to make it even easier. You may often find yourself fearful or upset about something in the moment without the time or ability to do a full clearing session. Times like these may include: sitting in traffic, waiting for a call you're nervous about, before work when you're short on time, and more. In these cases, a simpler version of EFT can be very beneficial. There is no reason to sit around and feel bad without clearing the energy at the same time.

How-To: The more formal process of using EFT involves creating and using a set-up statement to verbalize how you are feeling now, then going through the rest of the points while venting about that same thing. But if you're in a pinch, you can simply start tapping! If you're already feeling strong emotions because you are overwhelmed, something upsetting just happened, and so on, it's not so important to talk out loud because the energy is already right there and ready to be cleared. So simply feel all the feelings and tap through the rest of the EFT points to help neutralize that energy. Note: If you ever need to use this technique in a place where you're unable to tap on all of the points, simply put your hand in an inconspicuous place and tap on the fingertip points only.

Utilize Reminders from Your Past

Sometimes whatever is bothering you now is triggering you because it reminds you of the past. But it can be difficult to work on the past because it's just too scary—you don't recall details or are maybe too detached to conjure up the feelings in order to clear them. With this approach, you can simply ask, "When in my past did I feel this way?" When something pops into your head, try using tapping to work on those past feelings. Often, it will clear deeper energy than when tapping on current feelings.

How-To
REMINDERS FROM YOUR PAST

Think about a time or times from your past when you felt like you do now. Talk and tap on what you remember. Use any other means you can think of to bring up feelings associated with what you want to clear. These might include tapping while reading past journal entries aloud, writing out your story or feelings and then tapping as you read and reread them, recording your experience or feelings and tapping along to that, and playing songs from your past that evoke emotion so you can tap along.

Ask Your Subconscious Mind for Help

Calling on your subconscious mind for help is a great way to get some deep clearing, even if we don't know exactly what needs to be cleared. Remember, the subconscious mind knows everything.

How-To
ASK YOUR SUBCONSCIOUS MIND

Recite a short intention or prayer asking that your subconscious mind come to your rescue and help you clear. Something like the following will do just fine:

"I trust and allow my subconscious to help me clear this challenge. Thank you!"

An example set-up statement might look like this:

"Even though I have no idea what is making me feel so _____, I give my subconscious permission to release it anyway."

For the rest of the tapping points, focus on whatever issue you are clearing, trying to incorporate the emotions you feel and any information you have.

Tapping through these points might look something like this:

"I don't know what's making me anxious." "Maybe it's _____ (insert any guesses)." "My subconscious knows." "I just can't figure it out alone."

Just keep tapping and talking out loud, which will trigger your subconscious into pulling up whatever it needs to help you clear.

The more you practice using EFT, the more comfortable you'll become using it. And the more you use it, the more it'll help you find calm. There's no wrong way to do EFT, so go ahead and make it your own. Happy tapping to you!

CHAPTER 10

FIND PEACE THROUGH GOOD SLEEP PRACTICES

Angela A. Wix

Sleep is a foundation of health and wellbeing. Throw a wrench in that one detail and eventually the rest of life can end up feeling like it's coming undone. While sleep is important—vital, even—it's an area that many struggle with, myself included. Modern circumstances often set us up to always be monitoring, to be on the go, to be productive, to not miss out, and to do *more*. As a result, trying to downshift from "on" mode into a place where we can rest and recover can feel like an impossibility where sleep becomes a never-ending battle.

It should be easy: You set a time to go to bed every night and simply go to bed at that time. But stress and self-sabotage are two key obstacles to the simple goal of good sleep, and until they're called out directly, those obstacles can be hard to pin down. I know because this is an area of life I have long needed to attend to.

I'm a night owl by nature and can remember every summer as a teen finding myself naturally staying up past midnight and waking around 9 to 10 o'clock in the morning. Forcing myself into the hours of a schooltime regimen was brutal. Even as an adult, when I'm not setting an alarm or adjusting myself to the prescribed schedule of work and other life activities, I always sink back into my own natural timing. And if I'm not mindful, I might find myself still awake at 1, 2, and even 3 o'clock in the morning. When my late-night inclinations end up reducing my overall allotment or quality of sleep, it becomes a problem that ripples into every other area of my life.

Why is this even an issue? It took a long time for me to realize some of the reasons for my own sleep challenges. Sure, my personal internal clock clashing with a modern world played a role, but there's more that's wrapped up in it.

If you find yourself in the same boat, perhaps you also sometimes struggle with insomnia or painsomnia (sleep challenges caused by chronic pain). Because of this, subconsciously you might be staying up late in order to ensure you'll truly be tired and hopefully fall asleep more easily once you finally let yourself go to bed. Or maybe you simply don't like the feel of mornings. As a highly sensitive person this makes total sense to me, but I didn't realize until recently that part of my staying up and sleeping later has been a longtime subconscious way of avoiding that discomfort. Maybe you also find yourself practicing revenge bedtime procrastination, where you're unknowingly attempting to reclaim leisure time that you didn't get throughout your busy day.[1] If I'm stressed and procrastinating in other areas of my life, I find that revenge bedtime procrastination is much more likely to rear its head. Perhaps also like me, the mystery of the night is simply alluring to you. It's most naturally when my muse comes calling,

---

1. Eric Suni, "What Is 'Revenge Bedtime Procrastination'?" Sleep Foundation website, August 29, 2022, https://www.sleepfoundation.org/sleep-hygiene/revenge-bedtime-procrastination.

and I'm often inclined to follow those creative inspirations and leave sleep for later. These types of self-sabotage often become my norm, and it's not until I make an active choice to swing the pendulum the other way that I'm able to bring my sleep pattern back into balance.

These are just some examples of stressors, sleep issues, and self-sabotaging actions. Your natural sleep cycle and challenges for being well-rested may differ from mine, but no matter the specifics, there are common tools we can use to encourage balance around our sleep efforts. In the rest of this chapter, we'll focus on direct engagement. These are practices you can apply to set yourself up for success, including things like optimizing your sleep environment, defining your sleep challenges, and creating a sleep routine. We'll also look at how you can go about working through troubling dreams, stretches you can try for encouraging sleep, and spiritual practices that can be a great wind-down to the day. We'll conclude with a guided practice in relaxation and energy work to help you drift off into peaceful slumber.

For meditations, you can record and play it back, have someone read it to you, or read through and practice it by memory. As you read through these methods, have a journal handy so that you can jot down the things you plan on doing to improve your sleep hygiene. Alternately, you could use a highlighter to set off the example items that you're most drawn to applying yourself. Most of all, remember to be gentle with yourself. Instead of coming at these changes to your nighttime habits with a sense of strict duty, try to set your goals with curiosity. Find the techniques that work best for you and aim for gentle growth.

Practice

OPTIMIZE YOUR ENVIRONMENT FOR SLEEP

The first step in improving your sleep is to look at the practical details of your environment. Consider what's working and what's *not* working for you. Step into your space and tune in to the vibe it's giving off. Is it organized oasis or cluttered chaos? Start paying attention at night to what's actually disturbing you and make note of it. Think of this assessment as an edit. What needs to be erased or rewritten? Here are some examples:

- Declutter. Keep the space simple and clean, so that it feels like an escape and a place in which you can easily relax without distraction.
- Eliminate the TV and work. You want to program your body and mind so that it registers this room as a space for sleep instead of work or entertainment.
- Add white noise. If you're sensitive to noise or night-time quiet is too quiet, having a fan or white noise machine can be an absolute gamechanger.
- Have a humidifier if the air is too dry or a dehumidifier if it's too humid.
- Keep a cool temp at night. In the winter, keep the heat down while you sleep. In the summer if you don't have air conditioning, having a fan directed toward you can be helpful.
- Eliminate light. If you're extra sensitive, consider adding blackout curtains and exclude electronics. If you have a device, like your humidifier, that has an indicator light you can't turn off, put a sticker over it.

- Add more pillows if you need them. I use four!
- Have extra blankets within easy reach for weight and warmth.
- Make sure your mattress fits your needs. Soft, firm, adjustable, elevated, etc.
- Set an aromatherapy bottle by the bed as a reminder for use. Lavender and chamomile are popular essential oils for aiding sleep that you can inhale or spray in the space.
- Low lighting. Having dimmers or low light bulbs in the bedroom have a calming effect. Use lamps instead of overhead lights. Salt lamps are great for this purpose.
- Grounding sheets. Connecting to the earth's electric charge, known as earthing, may help to improve sleep. One way is using special sheets that connect to the ground that are plugged into an outlet.
- Separate room to sleep alone. Maybe you need to kick out the dog or cat from this particular room. If you have a partner whom you share a bed with, perhaps you'd sleep better in separate beds or even in separate rooms. While this is commonly thought of as a negative sign for the health of a relationship, that's actually a myth. In fact, it's a common practice. A survey by the Better Sleep Council showed that 63 percent of American couples choose to sleep separately for most of the night, and 1 in 4 sleep better when they're alone.[2] Alternately, maybe you would sleep best with

---

2. The Better Sleep Council, "Survey: American Couples Have Trouble in Bed: Sleeping Together Can Be a Nightmare For Couples," April 9, 2017, https://bettersleep.org/research/survey-american-couples-have-trouble-in-bed/.

the addition of a companion in your space. It's all individual. Do what works for you.

- What else would you add to this list?

Practice
Define Your Sleep Challenges

This is a next step to the previous practice in which we look at things that go beyond your physical setting that are working against your goal of good sleep. Take some time to tune in and think about what your reasons are for staying up late. What would your ideal sleep schedule be? Maybe being up late works for you, but if, like me, it sometimes becomes a problem, it's good to assess what's throwing you off. Also consider what might be keeping you from falling or staying asleep. What are the hurdles that you're running up against? Knowing them can make it easier to move beyond them. Examples of potential challenges and solutions include:

Problem: Taking naps during the day.

Solution: If you struggle with sleeping at night, it might be best to avoid naps, because they can end up hindering overall sleep. That said, you might find that you actually sleep best in shorter stretches, with a nap during the day and a portion of sleep during the night. This biphasic sleep schedule might be the way humans are programmed to most naturally sleep and may have been the norm prior to the industrial era.[3] It's usually considered a healthy practice so long as it works for you and you're still

---

3. Sarah Shoen, "Biphasic Sleep: What It Is and How It Works," Sleep Foundation, updated April 6, 2022, https://www.sleepfoundation.org/how-sleep-works/biphasic-sleep.

getting the total amount of sleep you need. I know someone who wakes very early in the morning for work, naps
when they get home if it feels like their body needs it, and
like clockwork goes to bed at the same time every night.
This routine works for them and as long as they don't
overdue the length of their post-work nap, they sleep fine
through the night. For others, a nap is absolutely a neces-
sity due to health issues. In order to be present for later-
in-the-day activities, they may require a midday nap to
refresh themselves. The key here is to know what works
for you. If you're fine with a 20- to 90-minute nap and it
doesn't disrupt the rest of your sleep needs, go for it.

Problem: Caffeine and other sleep-disrupting foods.

Solution: Addressing your diet can be an important
step in your goals for good sleep. Alcohol, caffeine, spices,
heavy meals, and food sensitivities or allergies can all act
as barriers. For me, wheat, chocolate, and foods that raise
my histamine levels are things that are guaranteed to give
me sleep issues. Eating too late can also be an issue. If you
aren't sure what might be causing a problem for you, try
keeping a food diary for a while and see if you notice a
pattern with what you eat in relation to the nights where
you struggle most with sleep.

Problem: Lack of activity.

Solution: Doing something active during the day
preps your body for rest later on. If you have a hard time
with increasing your physical activity, try taking a 10- to
20-minute walk a few days a week, increasing to 30 minutes, preferably every day. This is beneficial because any

exercise you do that day affects the quality of sleep you have that night.[4]

Problem: You're uncomfortable.

Solution: Think of this step as the Goldilocks detail. What's making you uncomfortable? Are you too hot or too cold? Is the bed too hard or too soft? Are you getting tangled in your night clothes? It can be surprising how powerful little tweaks aimed at your personal comfort can be. When I started looking closely, I realized my long hair was causing a problem; putting it in a braid before bed did the trick. I found that an extra soft blanket instead of sheets acts like a sleeping pill for me, and when the cooler weather allows for it, having the weight from a pile of comforters is heaven. I also need a soft mattress, a cool space, and a tank top instead of a nightgown or t-shirt.

Problem: You have loud roommates or neighbors, or you're simply a light sleeper.

Solution: Make use of white noise and earplugs. A simple fan (or fan app on my phone when I'm away from home) and Loop earplugs are my best friends when it comes to a good night's sleep!

Problem: You are distractable, engrossed in an activity, or lose track of time.

Solution: Set a bedtime alarm that will go off each night when it's time for you to start prepping for sleep.

---

4. John Hopkins Medicine, "Exercising for Better Sleep," https://www.hopkinsmedicine .org/health/wellness-and-prevention/exercising-for-better-sleep.

Problem: Sensitivity to EMFs (electromagnetic frequencies) or distraction of electronic media.

Solution: Set a time limit on your apps. For example, under Settings, my phone includes a digital wellbeing option along with its parental controls. Within this menu I can place a timer on each of my apps, and when I hit that time limit, the app pauses until the next day. You could also set an alarm on your phone and each day when it goes off, put your phone into airplane mode. This will disable its wireless features. Another option (one of my favorites) is to set a timer on your Wi-Fi so that it turns off at a certain time. Once it goes off, that's it for the day. This especially helps if you often find yourself mindlessly scrolling through social media. It's an extra cue that screentime is done and now is the time to go get ready for bed. Turning off Wi-Fi has the benefit of limiting EMFs. If you do have that sensitivity, it's also good to try eliminating other sources from your sleep area (desktop computer, laptop, tablet, phone, etc.) or unplugging them before you go to sleep.

Problem: Your circadian rhythm, or body clock, is out of sync. If you're struggling with insomnia, traveling to a different time zone, or are trying to shift your sleep time to a different range, your circadian rhythm might need a reset.

Solution: Instead of fighting against it, try being outside as the sun is setting so that your eyes take in the natural transition of light. Even better, get grounded at the same time. Connect your bare feet to the earth, touch a plant, or hold your bare hands to the ground to tap into the energy of the earth and help inform your body's internal clock. Getting outside or sitting by a light therapy box (sun lamps used for seasonal affective disorder) in the morning hours can also be helpful.

Problem: You're exposed to blue light in the evening or nighttime hours.[5] This one is guaranteed to act like caffeine for me and is also part of throwing off the circadian rhythm. If I'm in front of a computer in the hours after the sun has set I *will* have insomnia that night.

Solution: To counter this, you can set a red screen filter or night mode on your electronics. Found in your computer's display settings, this is sometimes called "night shift," "night mode," or "night light." It can be programmed to automatically turn on and off according to the time of day. I use an app on my Android phone called Twilight that does the trick. You can also get a blue light filter on your prescription glasses or purchase non-prescription blue light blocking glasses. It's also a good goal to end your screen time at least an hour before bed. Switching to an ambient amber-colored light bulb with no or low blue light in your bedroom for pre-sleep activities can also be very helpful.

Problem: You have a medical issue. Consider health issues that may be keeping you awake.

Solution: This is a rabbit hole that could lead to other possible issues, but with some detective work between you and your medical team, you might discover problems with accessible solution. For example, anxiety and depression are a couple of mental health issues that are connected to sleep problems. Perhaps you need to be assessed for sleep apnea to correct your breathing while you sleep.

---

5. Harvard Health Publishing, "Blue light has a dark side," July 7, 2020, https://www.health.harvard.edu/staying-healthy/blue-light-has-a-dark-side.

If you have chronic pain, you might need medical support for solutions when you're struggling with painsomnia. In my own case, I have mast cell issues and histamine intolerance, and when histamine levels are high, it can keep me awake. When I feel this is a problem, I take an antihistamine so that I have a better chance at falling to sleep. TMJ, a dysfunction of the jaw joint, is another example that wakes me throughout the night. Wearing a mouthguard allows me to avoid the uncomfortable clenching of my jaw and grinding of my teeth so that I can sleep more peacefully.

Problem: You have a fear of recurring nightmares.

Solution: If it's nightmares or other troubling dreams that are bothering you, you might need additional support beyond just trying to work things out yourself. Persistent nightmares for me are usually a sign that I need to work through underlying grief or trauma with a therapist, or that I need to better address symptoms of chronic illness with my medical team. If you decide to attempt working through this issue on your own, you could try the following practice.

Practice
ENERGETICALLY WORK THROUGH TROUBLING DREAMS

Nightmares and restless dreams can be a challenging issue and when they become a pattern, it can be extremely frustrating, but there are ways that you can use your intuition to help work through strong dream emotions.[6] When

6. Angela A. Wix, *The Secret Psychic* (Woodbury, MN: Llewellyn, 2022), 140–141.

you aren't sure what a dream is trying to get across to you or it's a persistent dream that you want to try to resolve, the practice of going back into the challenging dream can be very helpful. You do this while you're awake in order to actively process the dream's message, resolve distressing emotion, and dissolve the trauma that it triggered. In his book *Dreamworking*, Dr. Christopher Sowton calls this "re-enter and explore."[7] We'll do a form of this type of thing here. (Note: If it's too much to relive your triggering event, skip this and work with a professional to process your experience.) These are a few examples of how you can go about this type of practice:

- We all have a support system made up of those in spirit who are working to help us throughout our lives. Friends and loved ones who have passed on, as well as spirit guides who we might not be consciously familiar with, make up parts of this team. Ask that one of your guides be with you now to help you through this practice. See yourself and your guide as just witnessing and standing outside of the experience of your dream. Allow the details of the story to unfold for you. Notice what stands out the most. Focus in on the most triggering detail and ask it what it's trying to reveal to you. You might hear a message or see it transform into a different detail or an entirely new scene that plays out for you. Follow where the details lead. If you start to feel like you're going astray and the practice is becoming unfocused, bring yourself

---

7. Dr. Christopher Sowton, *Dreamworking* (Woodbury, MN: Llewellyn, 2017), 92.

back to the original starting point and focus again on a detail that you'd like explained.

- Another thing you can do is focus on that detail, give it light, and envision it transforming into something neutral or positive, like a venomous snake that turns into a flower or an attacker that turns into a snowman.

- You can also try adding in vocalization. This is a key aspect of talk therapy. I think of it as turning on the faucet of your throat chakra and allowing the buried well of your heart chakra to rise up and spill open. You might be surprised at how much this addition alone taps into and helps to release deeply buried emotions. As you go through playing out the details of the trauma, speak out loud to move that energy. Say what you're seeing or experiencing. If speaking to yourself feels too odd, ask your spirit helper to participate here with you. Say to them what you're noticing as the details play out, talking out the trauma with them as you go through it.

Once you've finished your practice, take some time to jot down the details. This can help you to process and resolve things even more.

Practice
CREATE YOUR SLEEP ROUTINE

Creating a sleep routine that works for you is another important step. Setting up a routine can help you connect with your circadian rhythm, clearly transition your day into night, and cue to your body and mind that you are safe and can relax.

Set Your Sleep Time

First, determine your optimum amount of sleep. From there, decide what time you plan to wake and then backtrack to figure out what time you need to go to sleep. For example, I need nine to ten hours of sleep: if I wake at 8 o'clock in the morning, I need to go to sleep ideally by 10 o'clock at night. Stick to your sleep time as much as possible, even on weekends. This helps to establish your sleep-wake cycle. Think of it as an exercise routine, but instead of working to build up muscle you're training your brain to be sleepy.

Tuck In Your Home for the Night

As you're winding down for the night, start writing out all of the things you're doing. Listing your end-of-day activities can help you clearly determine the length of time it takes for you to do all of these things. It can also keep you on track, ensuring that you aren't randomly adding in other things that might not be important for you to be dealing with before bed. Some of these list items might include:

- Turning off and putting away electronics
- Closing the curtains
- Turning the thermostat to a cooler temperature
- Putting kids and animal companions to bed for the night

- Tidying up any clutter that you want dealt with before bed
- Dimming and turning off lights

Decide On Your Pre-Sleep Activities

Aside from the obvious routine activities you're likely already doing (tucking the house in, brushing and flossing your teeth, going to the bathroom, putting on pajamas, setting your morning alarm, etc.,) decide what your bed-time wind-down activity options will be going forward. Think "no screen time" options and keep it fun so that it becomes something you can look forward to. These are also things you can turn to if you find yourself caught in a night of insomnia. Some ideas include:

- Reading a book or magazine
- Listening to an audio book or calming music
- Knitting, crocheting, or embroidery
- Activity books such as coloring, simple step-by-step drawing, Sudoku, connect-the-dot, crosswords, seek-and-find, or word search puzzles
- Journaling or writing down the next day's to-do list
- Praying
- Meditating
- Oracle or tarot reading
- Taking a bath
- Drinking a warm beverage. I've always found tea blends that include valerian root to be incredibly helpful for quality of sleep (consult with your medical professional to ensure you don't have any symptoms

or medical conditions that would cause this to be harmful for you).

- Gentle stretching

Practice
STRETCH TO ENCOURAGE SLEEP

When I do yoga, I tend to sleep much better. The following sequences are intended to help calm the nervous system down, tap into your breathing, and relax tension in the body to ease pain and discomfort. While I've practiced yoga for decades, I'm not a certified yoga instructor so I partnered with Shannon Yrizarry on these practices. Once I had the key poses and sequences set, she kindly provided the pose instruction to expertly guide you through your practice. We've shared two sequences here for you. The first is a full series for overall stretching, and the second is focused more on restoration.

*Sequence 1: Movement Sequence
for Overall Stretching*

This is a basic sequence that will help you to stretch various areas of the body.

Child's Pose (Balasana): Begin by sitting on your heels and bring your knees apart wider than your hips. Place your hands on the floor and slowly walk them forward until your forehead rests on the ground. Take five slow deep breaths in and out of your nose as you relax your body. To come out of the pose, gently lift your head as you inhale and walk your hands back up so you are upright. *It may be more comfortable* *to place a folded blanket over your heels for extra support in the pose.*

Cat-Cow Pose (Marjaryasana-Bitilasana): Come onto all fours with your hands as wide as your shoulders and your knees as wide as your hips. Your toes should be untucked so the tops of your feet are on the ground. As you inhale through your nose, point your tailbone up, drop the belly, and lift your chin for cow pose. Move fluidly into a rounded back as you exhale out of the nose and bring your chin toward your chest for cat pose. Move back and forth between cat and cow pose slowly five times and then return to a neutral spine position.

Cat Pose Variation Side Bend: Remain on your hands and knees in a tabletop position with your tailbone and head at the same height. Inhale slowly through your nose and turn your head to look down to the back and right. At the same time, push your left ribs to the left and you feel a stretch along the left side of the body. As you exhale, bring your gaze to the left and back as you push your ribs to the right and feel the stretch along the right side of the body. Move slowly between your left and right sides while breathing in and out of your nose, and then return to a neutral spine.

Downward Facing Dog Pose (Adho Mukha Svanasana): From tabletop position, tuck your toes and press into your hands as you lift your hips. Your body will make a triangle between yourself and the ground. Try to straighten your legs, bringing your heels toward the floor as you gaze back toward your legs. Keep your arms straight and fingers spread. Relax your neck and take five slow deep breaths in and out of your nose. Then gently bring your knees back to the ground.

Extended Puppy Pose (Uttana Shishosana): Bring your knees to the ground from downward facing dog and place your hands on the ground. Walk your hands forward and stack your hips directly over your knees. Keep your arms shoulder-distance apart with your palms facing down. Allow gravity to bring your chest closer toward the ground as you feel a stretch in your arms and shoulders. Take five slow deep breaths in and out of your nose, and then slowly walk your hands back up so they are under your shoulders to prepare for the next pose.

Downward Facing Dog Pose (Adho Mukha Svana-sana): Move back into downward facing dog by tucking your toes and lifting your hips as you straighten your legs. Take five slow deep breaths in and out of your nose.

Standing Forward Bend (Uttanasana): From downward facing dog, lift your head and look forward, keeping your hands on the floor. Slowly walk your feet forward toward your hands, breathing slowly as you transition. Bring your feet together directly under your hips into a standing forward bend, and relax the back of your neck so your head is able to hang heavily. Try to straighten your legs and reach to the outside of your legs behind you to grab your ankles or calves and pull your torso toward your thighs. Take five slow deep breaths in and out of your nose as you let gravity decompress your spine and you relax your back.

Palm Tree Pose/Upward Salute (Urdhva Hastasana): From standing forward bend, very very slowly so you don't get lightheaded, as you inhale, slowly circle your arms up as you bring your torso up into a standing position. Bring your palms together directly above your head in line with your spine and tilt your head back slightly to gaze at your hands. Continue to breathe slowly in and out of your nose five times as you slightly tuck the tail bone, put a micro-bend in the knees, relax your shoulders away from your ears, keep the arms in line with the ears, and keep your front ribs in.

Standing Forward Bend (Uttanasana): Swan dive with your arms as you bring your torso forward and come back into standing forward bend. Grab the back of your legs and pull your torso toward them with a relaxed neck as you take five slow and deep breaths in and out of your nose.

Downward Facing Dog Pose (Adho Mukha Svanasana): As you inhale, look up from forward bend and lean forward to place your hands on the ground. Walk your feet back so you come back into downward facing dog. Remain in this pose for five slow, deep breaths in and out of your nose. You can pick up your toes and spread them out, keep sinking your heels down, and bob the head to relax your neck.

Child's Pose (Balasana): From downward facing dog, bring your knees to the ground and walk your hands back so you can sit on your heels. Bring your knees wider than your hips and walk your hands forward so your forehead meets the ground. Continue to breathe slowly and deeply in and out of your nose and walk both hands slowly to the right. Take five slow and deep breaths in and out of the nose as you feel a stretch along the left side of the body. As you inhale, gently walk your hands back to the center and remain here for two breaths. Then walk your hands to the left so you feel a stretch along the right side of the body. Remain in this position for five deep breaths in and out of your nose. Relax your muscles more on each exhale. On an inhale, walk your hands back to center and take two slow, deep breaths here. Then walk your hands back up so you're sitting on your heels.

Squat/Garland Pose (Malasana): Place your palms on the ground and lift yourself onto your feet in a low squat. Place your elbows between your knees and press your palms together to help open the hips. Keep your spine upright so your tailbone points down. Eventually your heels will touch the ground. Spread your feet wider if it makes you more stable. Take five deep breaths in and out of your nose slowly, relaxing your body on each exhale.

Seated Forward Bend (Paschimottanasana): Come to a seated position with your legs together straight out in front of you. Inhale and lift your torso up, and exhale as you lean forward and reach your arms forward. Inhale and look forward straightening your spine in the bend and exhale relax into the forward bend letting go of all tension in the neck, back, and hips. Take five slow deep breaths in and out of your nose in this position. On an inhale, gently lift your torso upright. *If you have tight hamstrings, you can place a folded blanket under your hips to help you lean forward.*

Half Spinal Twist Pose (Vakrasana): Sit up with a tall spine and bring your right foot onto the ground outside of your left knee. Lift your left arm up and place your left elbow outside of your right knee. Place your right hand slightly behind you and use your lower stomach muscles to twist from the base of your spine to the right, keeping your spine tall. Let the ribs follow, then the shoulders and head without forcing with your left elbow. Take three slow, deep breaths here and then slowly unwind and repeat the same thing on the other side with your left foot outside the right knee.

Supine Spinal Twist (Supta Matsyendrasana): Gently lie on your back and hug your knees into your chest. Drop your knees to the right onto the ground and T your arms straight out to either side. To complete the twist, turn your head to the left. Take five deep breaths here in and out of your nose slowly. Bring yourself back to center and repeat the same thing on the other side, dropping your knees to the left. Relax into the pose more and more on each exhale.

Corpse Pose (Savasana): Straighten your legs out on the floor as you lie flat on the ground. Let your legs be slightly apart and allow your ankles to fall away from each other. Bring your arms slightly away from your body and relax your palms. Tuck your chin slightly to lengthen the back of the neck. Close your eyes and let your breath happen naturally. Consciously relax your muscles moving from the feet all the way to the top of the head as if you were butter melting over the floor. Remain here for seven to ten minutes and once you're done, start to move slowly, bring your knees into your chest and turn to the side to support yourself as you slowly sit up and take a moment to thank yourself for doing this practice that will improve your quality of sleep.

Sequence 2: Restorative Sequence for Drifting Off to Sleep

If you've ever been to a restorative yoga class, you'll know that many people nod off during these sessions. The experience is that wonderful! Included here are a handful of poses that are noted to be especially ideal for promoting stress relief, relaxation, and sleep. Feel free to do these as a sequence or choose one pose to sink into for a longer stretch.

Child's Pose (Balasana): Begin the sequence by sitting on your heels and bring your knees wider than your hips with your big toes still touching. Remain seated on your heels as your walk your hands forward on the ground and bring your forehead to the ground. For this sequence, instead of thinking about stretching, stop about 75 percent of the way there so that your muscles are able to stop gripping. Stay in this pose, breathing slowly and deeply, in and out of your mouth for 3 to 5 minutes. To stay in a relaxed state, get up very slowly and return to sitting upright.

Happy Baby Pose (Ananda Balasana): Gently lay yourself down onto your back and lift your legs up toward the ceiling. Hold the outsides or insides of your feet with bent legs and breathe slowly and deeply in an out of your nose, relaxing more on each exhale. Remain in happy baby for 3 to 5 minutes, and then hug your knees into your chest, gently rolling to the side and bringing yourself up to a seated position.

Seated Forward Bend (Paschimottanasana): Gently bring your legs out in front of you without forcing them straight but keep them together. Slowly lean forward and relax the back of your neck so your head just hangs. Don't worry about how far you stretch, just focus on slow deep breathing through your nose and relax more on each exhale. As you relax let your stress go with each exhale as well. Continue relaxing into the pose for 3 to 5 minutes. Very slowly, so you remain very calm, come back up to seated.

Legs-Up-the-Wall Pose (Viparita Karani): Slowly move toward a wall and sit with one side up against it. As you lean back, bring your legs up the wall so your torso is perpendicular to the wall. Rest your heels against the wall and bring your arms comfortably out to the sides with your palms facing up. Stay in the pose 3 to 5 minutes, breathing slowly and deeply—the breath is the most important part of every pose. Relax your hips, stomach, shoulders, and neck. When you're done, gently bring your legs to the side so you're in a fetal position, and wait here for a few breaths. Then slowly bring yourself up to seated without disturbing the very relaxed state you're in.

Reclining Bound Angle Pose (Supta Baddha Kona-sana): From a seated position bring the bottoms of your feet together with your knees out to the side. Gently lean back onto one elbow and then the other so you lie flat with the soles of the feet still together. It's okay if your knees don't touch the floor. Bring your arms out to the sides comfortably with your palms facing up. Breathe slowly and deeply in and out of your nose for 3 to 5 minutes. You could also put a pillow under each knee for a bit of extra support.

Corpse Pose (Savasana): You could move right into bed for this last pose or just straighten your legs out where you're lying on the floor. Let your ankles fall away from each other and allow your natural breath to happen. Relax each part of the body from your toes to your head, melting into the floor. Remain in corpse pose for 7 to 10 minutes to get the full rejuvenating effects.[8]

Practice
Connect with Spirit and Your Higher Self

Meditation and spiritual connection are excellent to practice after a physical practice like yoga. These practices offer a nice wind-down to the day. They can help calm

---

8. The Good Body, "8 of the Best Yoga Poses for Sleep: Nod off Faster and Wake up Fresher" May 10, 2022, https://www.thegoodbody.com/yoga-poses-for-sleep/.

your mind and body, get extraneous thoughts and intuitive messages out of your head, and sync you up with higher vibration, all to a calming effect. You can do all of these steps or pick one or two options to focus on.

Step 1: Sitting in the Power (Passive Practice)

Sitting in the Power is a practice based in mediumship that is all about letting go and connecting with the energy of Spirit.[9] It's a practice of surrendering where you're being still, sitting in quietness, and allowing yourself to feel sensations brought to you by that connection. My favorite instruction on Sitting in the Power (and what this practice is based on) comes from author and medium Michael Mayo, who describes it as a simple practice where you're becoming aware of your own energy and the atmosphere that's around you. These sensations might include tingling feelings, buzzing, a sense of heaviness or increased density, warmth or coolness, or feelings of deep relaxation and love.

The challenge here is accepting the fact that what you need to be doing is *not trying*. The less you try, the more you'll feel. Observe whatever comes to you as though they were clouds; the subtleties enter into your perception without engagement, and then you let them pass by. With each sensation, remind yourself to relax even more. Instead of grabbing onto the sensations, you're sinking even deeper into them.

---

9. Michael Mayo, "Module 1: Ethical Mediumship & Dispelling Myths & Fears" and "Module 2: Surrender as the Key to Mediumship," The Empowering Approach to Evidence-Based Mediumship (course). The Shift Network. June 2021.

Start by getting into a comfortable position and breath comfortably. Inhale and exhale, allowing your breath to ease you into a calm state. When thoughts come into your mind just observe and let go.

Become aware of the energy at your heart and what it feels like. Follow that energy. See where it moves and how it expands.

Continue to observe and sense the atmosphere around your body, feeling how it extends from your own energy.

Sit within this space, continuing to simply sense the energy in and around you, observing any sensations, and sensing the peace that comes to you.

Step 2: Download Your Intuitive Voicemails (Less Passive Practice)

This next step is a natural progression form Sitting in the Power.[10] Here, you're tapping into your own higher wisdom as well as messages from Spirit. I recommend doing this as part of your pre-sleep activities.

Start out by writing your to-do list for tomorrow. Consider it an info dump: jot down any thoughts you'd like to get out of your head. Writing will help your mind start to fully let go, making you less likely to have racing thoughts as you're trying to go to sleep.

Get comfortable now and take some deep breaths. As you focus on your breathing and allow it to deepen, progressively relax all areas of your body, moving from your feet and legs, up to your torso, arms, hands, on up to your neck and head.

---

10. Wix, *The Secret Psychic*, 130–131.

When you feel settled in, tune in and ask your intuition to reveal any messages it's holding for you. Don't force it or try to engage—just allow the details to naturally rise into your awareness, noticing what you hear, see, and feel.

As you would when taking a phone message, jot down the key details shared with you. After you receive your messages, you can end the meditation. Or, if you want, you can ask any questions you might have about the details you just received and end when you feel the responses winding down.

Step 3: Oracle or Tarot Spread (Active Practice)

If there's anything you want further clarification on, you can do a reading with an oracle or tarot deck. I like to pull a single card or a sequence of three cards and continue in the way of step two. Connect with intuitive guidance (thoughts, imagery, or sensations that come to you) and see how the visuals and meaning of the cards continue to clarify that message.

Practice
GUIDED MEDITATION AND ENERGY WORK FOR RELAXATION AND SLEEP

This last practice is the perfect one for us to end on, as it's great to do before bed or as you're drifting off to sleep.[11] It incorporates muscle relaxation with a bit of energy work.

Take a moment to settle comfortably into your space. You can practice this meditation sitting or lying down. If you fall asleep, that's okay. Take some deep breaths now and consciously relax.

---

11. Wix, *The Secret Psychic*, 23–25.

Relax your feet, your calves, your upper legs. Moving up, now relax your hips. Take another deep breath and feel it filling your belly. Relax your abdomen. Relax your chest. Continue to move up, feeling the tension release from your neck. This relaxing sensation trickles down through your arms and into your hands. It spreads into your face now, and you feel your jaw, your lips, and the muscles around your eyes and in your forehead all relaxing. Take another deep breath now and feel your body melting even more into the surface that's gently supporting you.

Sit in this relaxed state for a moment.

When you're ready, rest one hand on your heart and the other on your belly. Feel the energy in your hands. You might sense it as movement or a thickening sensation in the space at your palms. See this energy as a vibrant light. It moves from your hands into your heart space and abdomen. Feel the warmth as it fills your body and expands out to your limbs and up to your head.

Savor this sensation for a bit before moving on.

In your mind's eye now, see yourself standing at the top of a set of stone stairs. With your bare feet, take a step down, then another, and another. The stones are rough underfoot and the air that was initially warm starts to feel damp and cool. You run your hand along the mossy stone walls as you continue making your way down. With each step, it's as if you're removing the weight of the day from your shoulders. The stairs continue downward, until the sunlight from above is almost entirely out of sight. Finally, you reach the bottom, feeling light and free.

There you find a door and looking at it you know there is something *fantastic* waiting for you on the other side. You take a step forward and wrap your hand around the cool knob, turn it, and swing the door open. On the other side you find a luxurious space for relaxation. Perhaps it's a beach with turquoise waters. Maybe it's a reading nook stacked with pillows, blankets, and books with a window revealing a drizzly autumn day. Or it could be a giant bed topped with cozy comforters, ready to envelop you. Wherever you find yourself, move fully into your space and take it all in.

As you're getting ready to sit down in your space, you notice a small table with a beautiful box sitting on it. Step closer and look at the details of this box. You pick it up, turn it over in your hands, and open it to see that it's empty, waiting for you to fill it. Set it back on the table and take a deep breath. Once again feel your muscles relaxing all over and ask that any remaining tension be released. Any pain and discomfort you have rises up and away from you, like steam into the air. See it form into a bubble and then solidify further into a gemstone. It hovers in the air in front of you until you take it and place it in the box, where you then close the lid. The box and its contents disappear and are no longer your concern. Take another deep breath and feel the lightness that remains in your energy and body.

Now fully immerse yourself into your space. Sit in your nook and watch the rain falling, the wind blowing in the trees. Sit on your beach and listen to gentle waves rolling in. Dive into that bed and feel yourself sink deeply into the folds of its embrace. Whatever your space looks like, sink into it.

Take all the time you need to enjoy this moment of relaxation.

If you choose to drift off to sleep from here, you're welcome to. If you decide you want to make your way back into the day, see yourself stepping away from your lovely space and know that it will be here waiting for you whenever you decide to return.

Move back through the doorway now and, without looking back, sense the door close behind you. Now move up, up, up, and back into the daylight ahead.

Take a moment to get yourself back into the present moment. Feel your body. Wiggle your fingers and toes and take a good stretch. Drink a glass of water. If you'd like, jot down the details of your experience in your journal.

I hope within these different methods you found some options that help you unwind from the daily stresses of life so you can rest easily throughout your nights. As you continue your efforts toward improved sleep hygiene, may each method leave you waking refreshed and ready to meet your days.

CHAPTER 11

The Calming Effects of ASMR

Shannon Yrizarry

Please note that ASMR (autonomous sensory meridian response) is not meant to treat any serious psychological or physical disorder. In rare cases, ASMR may cause anxiety. It may be due to a fight-or-flight response in the autonomous nervous system called misophonia. If you notice your heart rate rising, discontinue use of ASMR. If you know you have strong negative reactions to specific sounds, there are many other calming techniques you can use in other chapters of this book. The author and publisher are not liable for any reactions a reader may have to ASMR. It is advisable to consult with your physician before using ASMR or if you find it doesn't produce positive effects.

If you haven't heard of ASMR, you're not alone. Most people have only a vague idea of it through social media, and that idea is somewhere between extremely satisfying viral videos and maybe a video showing the crunching of paper bags. It is so much more than that!

ASMR incorporates audio and visual media that cause what has come to be known as brain tingles. You can also learn to be more aware with your senses without these tools and achieve the effect which is also referred to as a brain orgasm. This is a sensation that calms your body and feels, well, you'll have to just experience it for yourself. The microphones used for ASMR pick up the most faint sounds and amplify them. You may be surprised at the sounds you never thought about that give you brain tingles!

Examples of some of the many different types of ASMR include: folding towels, mixing paint, people eating food, slime videos, crinkling things such as a paper bag, watching someone's hair get cut, listening to role play, listening to whispering that sounds sweet and nurturing, fingers tapping gently, someone combing their hair, blowing sounds, pencils writing on paper, and lighting arrangements.

In the ASMR community, viewers and content makers use the word "trigger" to refer to what creates tingles or what just puts you to sleep. Some content makers include many triggers in their videos, which can be up to three hours long.

There are videos that make you feel nurtured and seen where the ASMRist looks right into the screen and even puts their hand on it. This triggers an experience of feeling like you're socializing in a comforting way, which can be good to help with feelings of isolation.

ASMR is included in this book for a reason—the topic actually spurred the idea for the entire book, which came from the amazing author Angela A. Wix. You'll notice this chapter is casual, like we are having a conversation. Forget the face-scrunching idea of complexity … let's enjoy this little chat and have some fun!

Welcome to what may ostensibly be the weirdest chapter in this book. While you are learning to access different states of consciousness with many of these esteemed authors, this topic of ASMR is so new that meditators may dismiss it as something that is not as valid as the tried-and-true meditation techniques that have been around much longer.

With that being said, open your mind to the possibility that this technique may be just what your body needs. That's right. The monkey mind makes us feel anxious and it's hard to shut off, but the body is the gateway to freeing yourself from that chaotic state.

For many people, it's hard to find time to get to savasana with a full yoga class every day. Body relaxation takes about seven minutes at the end of class, and you have about three minutes of relaxation if students aren't already getting up while missing the best part of class.

But hey, no judgment. Yoga itself has become more of a workout than a way to tap into that bewildering, elusive, magical state of nirvana. The state of relaxation is not something to discount because it bypasses thinking about thinking. There are so many distractions roaming in our minds that accessing calm is most accessible through, you guessed it, the body.

Since we can't always do a full yoga class and when we meditate, we often think about how we aren't good at meditating and/or fall asleep, we can look to this new and scientifically studied tool that is quick, rejuvenating, and doesn't require doing something.

Relaxation is the opposite of doing, and yet many of us relate the concept to something we must do that causes more stress. Let's emphasize the point that relaxation only arrives when we surrender to not doing anything. We must trust that letting go will allow us to reach a state more valuable than even the most delicious pumpkin bread, which is undeniable proof that there is a higher power.

Now let's dive into ASMR in a simple and fun way. This is not some hard-to-comprehend, years-of-studying, vague and arduous path—it is already all there for you. It's delightful and doesn't cost you anything but a few minutes. This is going to be fun, easy, and you can experience it today.

Before we get into this goodness like the mental cupcake it is, we are going to solidify how cool the effects of ASMR truly are. We aren't joining a cult or paying into some pyramid scheme promising peace—instead we are looking at a fun topic that will help us in the most significant areas of life we are looking to improve.

The Benefits of ASMR

Feeling calm will offer higher levels of happiness, energy, and intuition than any other way we try to push these things into our reality. It's counterintuitive because we are conditioned to believe that success comes from hard work, happiness comes from fulfilling our dreams, and energy comes from self-punishing exercise. Let go all of those ideas and step over to the wild side where being calm will allow you to experience the secret elixir of life. This is totally a real thing. We don't need to look at all the typical physical effects touted by each new superfood or herbal tea.

What we want is to expose the energy that can only be experienced and not commonly understood. You will become healthier but what you really get through calmness, no matter what chapter in this book you use, is something much more powerful in gentle and unexpected ways.

Power is not always about shooting fire out of your eyes to save the world like a Marvel character or being so confident that you lead a company. Power is having the ability to see what will give you happiness beyond what society dictates.

Energetic Experiences
You Can Expect Using ASMR

- A sense of knowing that the way you've been thinking has been draining you and is not allowing you to be comfortable in your own skin.
- A release of negative heavy energy you've been processing in your body picked up from other people's problems.
- You feel your chest expand and feel like you can breathe when your body finally relaxes.
- A realization that you can let go of anything or anyone that doesn't make you feel safe, supported, and loved.
- You do not need to *create* peace because pausing and being sensitive to what you naturally are shows you what the body gives you in this state.
- An expanded state of self in which you are aware of the energy you can track to continue to stay in this state of calm.
- The ability to discern which action feels right, heightened by tapping into a relaxed sensory state you're getting to know that allows you to avoid major detours in your path to sustained happiness, e.g., a job where you will be mistreated.
- New ways of looking at things that we perceive as problems. When we relax, our natural creativity kicks in so we see a perceived obstacle as the solution we need to open to a more empowered way to hold on to our calm without attaching it to outcomes.
- Creative ideas that appear using your third eye as a sense of knowing or a burst of inspiration. This allows you to shift into a state of creating opportunities instead of going

along with other people's momentum which may or may not suit you.

- You can sense what you really want out of life and what you feel is purposeful to your unique soul blueprint.
- The ability to sense things before they happen, allowing you to be prepared, in addition to being able to sense what people are feeling so you can navigate situations more intelligently.
- Practicing calm makes you a calmer person throughout the day, easier and more pleasant to be around, and open to possibilities for relationships that can change your life. You'll begin to manifest calm around you. Think about that. Focusing on calmness will manifest more of it in your life.

These are some deep benefits that are often pushed aside because we don't believe we can get them. We are in a world where we are trained to use reason and logic over our sensory experiences, which don't require the same process of using the mind but allow us to expand our consciousness to feel energy and frequencies that provide information in a way that is not about numbers and appearance but about how you feel and how to navigate toward better energy.

Of course, we still deal with stress from daily life, so we can look at the more commonly associated ideas of the benefits we want.

Mental Health and Physical Health Benefits of ASMR

- Helpful for insomnia and falling asleep
- An easily accessible antidote for anxiety
- Lowers stress, which helps bolster your immune system
- Reduces depression

- Helps lower your heart rate
- Has a therapeutic effect by producing positive emotions

Philosophy Around Pleasure

While meditation can be practiced without much judgment in today's modern age (even if it is called mindfulness), ASMR may raise more eyebrows. The sights and sounds are not what we are used to, and the idea of pleasure has been widely suppressed when it comes to direct sensory experiences that are termed orgasmic.

While society is accepting of the pleasure of food, amusement parks, movies, and music, things that trigger a physiological response in the body may generate subconscious shame within ourselves. For example, many families feel uncomfortable talking about subjects that provide pleasure and prefer to let those topics remain behind closed doors. Similarly, in social situations, talking about pleasure can be awkward and frowned upon.

Looking back to the origins of the suppression of pleasure can unwind our own resistance to it. There are a variety of belief systems that associate the desires of the body and bring us further away from spiritual connection. Celibacy, chastity, and covering the body in public have been a part of many cultures and still are, even as we see perspectives on these topics evolve lethargically. Why bring this up? It could keep you from taking that step to either try this for yourself or share it with someone else.

Because there are many videos that include whispering and other intimate and sensual experiences, we may avoid the very media that could provide us the most immersive experience. These sensory experiences bring us fully into the present so that we stop worrying about the future and the past. They allow the relaxation of the body because they stop our thoughts.

These videos may help us relax, but let's be perfectly clear: this experience is *not* sexual; the feeling produced by ASMR is in the brain. Nonetheless, in order to get fully immersed into ASMR media, we must have something that really is, as scary as this word may be, pleasurable.

We can look to the practice of yoga as a parallel to our own actions in response to our immediate or community pressures. Some of us may have been chastised for practicing yoga because it seems personally indulgent. Perhaps we have been criticized for doing poses that are inadvertently sexual. However, those who practice yoga know that in order to do the poses while monitoring the breath and moving into another pose, it requires all of one's focus. We cannot focus on the past, present, or future worries…unless we want to fall over. This focus allows the mind to be fully immersed in the present and give us a break from fight-or-flight feelings.

When we are fully in the present, we become aware of what our body is feeling, which is a direct line to our intuition. Whether it's yoga, ASMR, or something as simple as wearing a favorite outfit, eventually we will experience this deeply ingrained feeling of shame whether we are projecting it onto ourselves or being the receivers of shaming from others.

Yogic philosophy aims to help one notice the positive and negative minds through the practice of being present. In many ways, ASMR is a form of meditation just as valid as walking, drawing, or eating can be.

As we notice our judgments within our own minds, we start to empower ourselves to detach from the rollercoaster of good and bad. ASMR can be a tool to help us access the neutral mind. When watching an ASMR video, are we judging them as good or bad? Can we notice these more quiet thoughts?

The neutral mind allows us to stay calm. It allows us to see things from a bird's-eye view and not get caught up in petty drama or euphoria that can result in a crash of dopamine. This neutral mind is the entire goal of the very arduous process of yoga. ASMR could be a faster link to this neutral mind that we will call "peace" for all practical purposes.

The philosophy that allows the sensations of the body to be ignored does not allow us to embrace who we fully are, which is where peace lies. If we deny part of ourselves, we will not inherently feel that we are free, which also is peace.

Now that we have addressed why we may avoid this newfangled ASMR trend, let's get into how it works and how to do it.

How It Works

Sound and sight are vibrations, wavelengths that move energy in our body in both a physical and responsive way. Auditory wavelengths create harmony in our energy where there is discord.

Sound is used in many spiritual systems that people can use to feel a state of calm. Hymns, gongs, incantations, meditation music, and mantras all generate a physical release of tension in the body like a massage.

Colors create responses that generate certain feelings and shift us from a state of fight-or-flight to rest and relax. Colors also create a wavelength that interacts with our body to alleviate pressure in the psyche, tension in the muscles, and racing thoughts that wreak havoc on our ability to tap into that intuitive state. To understand how colors help to stimulate relaxation in the body, we can look to the ancient Sanskrit chakra system that correlates colors to certain emotions. Similarly, we can notice what colors make us feel calm and relaxed, which may help us in choosing which ASMR videos we might like.

Certain sounds can generate certain emotions or colors in our mind's eye. Even an audio-only ASMR relaxation recording can give you the feelings colors bring you and are usable anywhere and everywhere.

We are going to briefly skim the science but not in a make-you-snooze way. This chapter is about giving you the power to feel calm and tap into your intuition, not make you a scientist.

The most important thing to know is that ASMR releases chemicals that make us feel good. MRI scans of the brain reveal which parts are engaged while watching ASMR videos. The brain activates in a variety of places that reveal a new type of response scientists are not used to explaining, perhaps because many ASMR experiences come from a technology-based source. However, many people have experienced this tingling their whole lives without having a name for it. The body feels a mix of comfort and excitement that almost seem to counter each other. This phenomenon is still relatively new, and more studies are being done.

The cool part is that in the digital sphere, we are finding new ways to feel good and enhance intuition and don't need drugs to get there. Many people are now even taking ASMR seriously as a career.

Research on using ASMR for many different applications is already being done. Notably, a scientific article written by Diana Bogueva and Dora Marinova titled "Autonomous Sensory Meridian Response (ASMR) for Responding to Climate Change," published in 2020, discusses the applications of using ASMR to positively influence behaviors to take care of the environment instead of fear-based news.[1]

---

1. Diana Bogueva and Dora Marinova, "Autonomous Sensory Meridian Response (ASMR) for Responding to Climate Change." Curtin University Sustainability Policy (CUSP) Institute. Curtin University. Vol. 12, Issue 17. August 26, 2020. Accessed October 19, 2022, www.mdpi.com/2071-1050/12/17/6947.

Try It for Yourself

With more than 13 million ASMR videos on YouTube with an estimated 5.7 trillion views, a newbie can look to the top-ranking ASMR videos to dip their toe into this tingly ocean. Considering ASMR really came about in 2007, it has seriously exploded across the internet.

ASMR does not have to come from a video—it can be produced from your surroundings and from listening to something. As you feel these warm tingles come down from the top of your head, you'll notice that a variety of things can trigger you to feel this way. There is a huge variety of options so if you're not digging one, you have millions more to pique your interest. As of 2022, here are some of the most-loved ASMR channels on YouTube to get you started.

Olivia Kissper is one the most well-known ASMRists online. Her videos on YouTube have more than 22 million views. She combines hypnosis techniques, guided and visual meditative experiences, and ASMR. With a soothing voice, she focuses on helping people fall asleep and find the peace of having no thoughts. She even wrote a book called *How to Achieve Nothing: 3-Step Time Reversal Formula to End Stress, Overwhelm and the Strategizing Mania* for type-A productive personalities that expands upon the value of finding nothing. Her techniques of bringing viewers to a state of nothing reflect what practitioners aim to achieve in Buddhist meditation. You can find her videos at https://www.youtube .com/c/OliviaKissperASMR. Check out her video with over 2 million views, entitled "WARNING! This ASMR Will Get You High— Mega Brain Tingles Psychedelic Experiment Role Play." It runs just under half an hour.

Dennis ASMR, a rare male ASMRist, is a younger personality who provides videos for insomniacs. His passion for helping people sleep brings a range of colorful videos usually against a black background. His videos focus on whispering and mouth sounds. He has role-play videos where he is a doctor and an Uber driver on a rainy day, and there are many types of sticky, foamy, funky things that provide tingles when touched to the microphone. ASMR is dominated by women, and Dennis has broken the mold with over a million followers. One of his most watched videos with over 16 million views is called "99.9% of YOU will sleep to this ASMR video." Find his channel at: https://www.youtube.com/c/DennisASMRYT.

WhispersRed has a soothing British accent that is nurturing and motherly. She even has videos for kids to help them fall asleep and calm down. She likes to tell stories but also offers videos that have no vocals. She is an ASMR veteran and has experienced tingles her whole life. This channel is great for ASMR newbies because she is easy to listen to and knows triggers from years of personal experience. She has more than a million subscribers to her channel: https://www.youtube.com/c/WhispersRedASMR. To get started, check out her popular video with more than 12 million views: "22 ASMR Triggers | No Talking | Intensely Relaxing Sounds."

SAS-ASMR offers unique videos mostly focused on food. Her colorful videos show her eating things such as mochi, noodles, fruit, honeycomb, and more. She captures the sound of eating, which her 9.37 million subscribers find relaxing. She encourages wearing headphones and is known for the Korean internet phenomenon known as *mukbang*, in which people eat food and are filmed as though you are sharing a meal with them. You can find her channel at: https://www.youtube.com/c/SASASMR. One from 2018, with more than 50 million views, is called "ASMR HONEYCOMB (Extremely STICKY Satisfying EATING SOUNDS) NO TALKING | SAS-ASMR *PART 2*."

Tom Slime is the slime guy. He's not the only one, but he does slime well, having 9.22 million followers. The slime colors are vibrant, and the slow movement and mixing of slimes with different sparkles and opacities is weirdly satisfying. There is a wide variety of slime videos on his channel that involve other objects and playfulness as well. It certainly awakens the kid in us, helping us remember a time when we were able to play and be fully present. Check it out for yourself: https://www.youtube.com/c/VickyCoolTV. And if you want to see one of—if not the most—popular videos (732 million views), watch "Mixing Store Bought Slime Into Clear Slime–Most Satisfying Videos."

In addition to YouTube, there are other resources for ASMR videos and audio recordings. There are ASMR apps such as Tingles, ASMRtist, TeasEar, and Mindwell, and you can purchase ASMR audio recordings on iTunes and Spotify. If you are a hands-on person, you can also make your own ASMR recordings to let your creativity soar. There are lots of ASMR kits on Amazon.com, as well as instructional videos about how to use the equipment and make the special trigger effects.

You can also train yourself to use your environment to generate ASMR. Turning on your six senses and noticing sounds, colors, textures, movements, physical sensations (such as the bass from a stereo), and the space between these things your senses pick up can generate this for you.

Notice how you feel when you see something your brain finds interesting, even something as simple as a pattern. Allow yourself to open all your senses at once as if you're taking every sensation in all at once.

Sensory awareness also greatly enhances intuition. As you're entirely immersed in the moment, worry and stress melt away. Don't worry about finding the right thing to focus on. Don't focus on anything—let your curiosity lead you as you become completely relaxed.

How to Intuitively Use ASMR to Be Calm

This entire book is about how to listen to your body and the energy you sense to know what you need in order to stop anxiety, become clear headed, and be able to enjoy life, wherever you may find yourself.

In order to know when and which ASMR video will be helpful, it's good to prepare yourself and be aware of your anxiety triggers so you can stop and listen to your body throughout the day.

The perfect time to give yourself the gift of relaxation is when you are faced with big decisions. Not only will you feel better, you'll also be able to tap into your gut instead of overthinking the decisions. We get anxious when we have a lot of little decisions to make because we are busy or are used to doing a lot in a day. If we don't listen to it, this background anxiety can make us sick because the body is smart enough to make us slow down.

Before we get sick, it's helpful to create a habit of checking in with your body and emotions to see how you're feeling. If you are scattered, ASMR will help balance your energy. If you are feeling depressed, ASMR can help your brain release happy chemicals, and your mind can follow the body's energetic cue as you get that ASMR pick-me-up.

You can plan to do ASMR at night before bed if you have trouble falling asleep. If you struggle with anxiety throughout the day, start your day with ASMR. Dealing with anxiety is just as important as brushing your teeth.

Even a quick fifteen-minute break can stop you from having a bad day and keep you in a good mood. If you find yourself speaking negatively with others, ASMR could really help you to shift your energy and break out of that negative wavelength.

When you feel your mind is all over the place and you find it hard to focus, scrambling can steal your energy and lower your cognitive bandwidth, making you very inefficient. Using ASMR can help you have more mental energy without the chaos. The next time you're feeling overwhelmed with information and don't know what to do first, seriously, try it.

How to Know Which ASMR Is Best for You

This is where many of us can feel analysis paralysis. If you find yourself scrolling through Netflix more than actually watching something, you may find yourself doing the same with ASMR videos. The goal of using ASMR is to get in touch with what your body and your energy is asking of you. Your intuition knows much more than your mind does about what you need at any given moment.

One great way to tune in to what will help you is to not overthink it. You're just tapping into a direction. Sit quietly, away from distractions if possible, see what images or sounds come to mind, then search for those words and ASMR videos. It's as simple as that.

For example, if you're at work and feeling like you have too much on your plate, you can find a quiet place and close your eyes. As you take deep breaths, set the intention to be drawn to a video that will help you with this specific moment. You may think about a video you've seen pop up or even a type of voice might come to mind.

If you know you're dealing with a specific feeling or emotion such as fear or sadness, search for an ASMR video to help with the specific type of feeling bothering you. Rest assured that others out there are looking for the same thing, which is by itself nice to know, that we all deal with this type of thing. You can also search for a video that provides the opposite of your current feeling, such as happiness and peace.

Depending on what you're dealing with, another way to intuitively choose which ASMR video or recording will help you at a specific time is to scroll through the videos and notice if one pops out and seems to resonate with you. Notice if you feel as though a female or male energy would be more comforting or if you'd like a simple sound instead of a voice. If you talk and listen to people all day, something very different may be just what you need.

We each have the ability to tap into our intuition to find what will balance and enhance our energy from the level of our soul, which is a magical and amazing superpower that gets stronger the more it is used.

You may be wondering: "What's the catch?" While science hasn't given a definitive explanation, it does seem that not everyone experiences ASMR. Perhaps this is because they are hardwired to enjoy the pressure of stress, or maybe they aren't fully focusing on the sensory input. ASMR is not a one-size-fits-all solution for feeling calm. The therapeutic benefits will depend on many factors. If this sort of sensory tool doesn't appeal to you, you can utilize the other wonderful techniques in this book. You can always ask questions in the comments section of ASMR YouTube videos and read what other people are posting there to get tips for beginners.

When it comes to things such as meditation or getting a massage, it's commonly accepted that people with experience can produce a better physiological response, which is why there are classes on these topics. In this new frontier of ASMR, don't give up and don't put pressure on yourself to get the feeling right away. Remember that most people new to meditation aren't able to go into deep states of consciousness for a while either. Luckily, ASMR can work right away. It also has been shown to lower the heart rate as much as relaxing through mindfulness practices and listening to calming music.

In conclusion, dear friends, sweet humans, and beautiful souls, calmness opens the doors to mystical knowledge. Trust in yourself, in the happiness you generate, and in your ability to heal others.

Bibliography

Bogueva, Diana, and Dora Marinova. "Autonomous Sensory Meridian Response (ASMR) for Responding to Climate Change" in *Sustainability* 12, no. 17 (2022): 6947. https://doi.org/10.3390/su12176947.

Brain Tingles: The Physiological Benefits of ASMR. Neuroscience-News. Retrieved July 3, 2022. https://neurosciencenews.com/asmr-physiology-9426/.

Cummins, Eleanor. "Why ASMR Calms Some People Down and Sends Others into a Rage." *Popular Science* website, January 29, 2021. https://www.popsci.com/story/science/asmr-misophonia-videos/.

Mayer, Melissa. "Testing the Tingles: The Science Behind ASMR." BrainFacts website. February 2, 2021. https://www.brainfacts.org/thinking-sensing-and-behaving/emotions-stress-and-anxiety/2021/testing-the-tingles-the-science-behind-asmr-020221.

Poerio, Giulia Lara, Emma Blakey, Thomas J. Hostler, and Theresa Veltri. "More than a feeling: Autonomous sensory meridian response (ASMR) is characterized by reliable changes in affect and physiology" in *PLoS One* 13(6), April 17, 2018: https://doi.org/10.1371/journal.pone.0196645.

Richard, Craig. "Mental Health Benefits of ASMR: The Research and Application." Video conference, May 17, 2022: https://www.marylandpsychology.org/mental-health-benefits-of-asmr--the-research-and-application.

Sharkey, Lauren. "28 ASMR Triggers for Anxiety Relief, Sleep, and More." Healthline website, September 19, 2019. https://www.healthline.com/health/asmr-triggers.

Sizelove, Valerie. "10 Best ASMR YouTube Channels to Subscribe to in 2022." Retrieved July 3, 2022. https://mellowed.com/best-asmr-youtube-channels/.

CHAPTER 12

Amplifying Joy and Gratitude Through Mindfulness

Melanie C. Klein with Marc Cordon

Gratitude and joy are powerful building blocks for creating and enjoying a satisfying, fulfilling, and expansive life. The most exquisite, dynamic, and powerful partnership we've experienced, gratitude and joy together have brought huge wins into every aspect of our lives. They go together like peanut butter and jelly or hot sauce and wings, whether you go for chicken or the vegan version.

The more we recognize all we have to be grateful for in our lives, the more joy we invite into our lives. The more joy we make space for each day, the more deeply we feel gratitude. It's a powerhouse pairing that has the potency to change your inner world radically. And when it does? The experience of the outer world shifts in tandem.

Gratitude and joy aren't the end goal. Gratitude and joy are a tool, a medium, a method. In short, gratitude and joy are the path.

Ready to Walk with Us?

Do you feel stressed out, anxious, or frustrated by life? Do you ever feel like your to-do list is never-ending? Are you completely stressed out about having too much on your plate that you can handle at once? If so, you might be headed for overwhelm.

It happens to the best of us when there are too many demands and expectations and the pressure to meet them are too much. Overwhelm is a legitimate emotional response to stress, and not just from external factors like a demanding job or family obligations. That's because most of us are biologically predisposed to respond emotionally in situations where we feel pressured by demands that don't match our own resources or ability to meet them. What this means for the average person is that there are ways we can deal with overwhelm other than shutting down and hiding away from the world. The absence of overwhelm does not necessarily mean the presence and expansiveness that come with joy and gratitude, but by cultivating mindfulness through a variety of tools and practices, we can lower the feeling of overwhelm and use the same tools proactively to convert positive outcomes and gratefulness through mindfulness.

What Is Mindfulness?

Mindfulness is a state of attentiveness and awareness toward what is happening in the present moment. It means being conscious of your thoughts, emotions, and physical sensations without judgment or criticism. It is about doing what you need to do when you need to do it without overthinking or planning. Focusing on the present can help people stay grounded and stop the tendency to analyze everything around them. For people who feel overwhelmed by life, this offers a helpful tool for staying sane.

Mindfulness is not about escapism, ignoring your problems, checking out, or leaving it up to the universe. It is a practice that can help you learn how to be more mindful and allow you to live in a state of presence rather than reactivity and fear. Rather than running away from a situation, mindful practices promote engaging and experiencing the moment fully and making space for yourself in an often hectic world. Conscious people are more self-aware, focused, and able to deal with difficult emotions like anger, frustration, or sadness. That's a clear link to the ability to choose, cultivate, and nourish gratitude and joy in your life sustainably throughout your life and everything that goes with being human.

Mindfulness is a lifestyle and way of being. For gratitude and joy to truly work their magic in your life, it's important to embody them and not just understand them. Mindfulness is accessible to anyone and everyone as a way to improve their mental, emotional, and physical health to positively affect their overall well-being. It can be as simple as taking deep breaths, focusing on your body in the present moment, or observing your thoughts without getting caught up in them.

The Key to Opening
Up Space and Possibility

To access all the goodness we've offered as a possibility in your own life through mindfulness, one thing must be noted. You must observe and accept what happens in your life without judgment and powerfully accept what is right now. Our attuned awareness allows us to flip the switch to "off" when it comes to riding the emotional roller coaster, taxing our nervous system, and spinning out.

One of the most important benefits of mindfulness is that it strengthens our ability to deal with stress, especially with the heightened worldwide stressors we're faced with in modern times. This ability becomes especially evident when we put mindfulness into action during challenging situations like when we are overwhelmed. Focusing on one thing at a time can help avoid getting too consumed by life's obstacles, challenges, and disappointments.

In addition to strengthening our ability to cope with stress, mindfulness has many other benefits, such as improved attention span and memory, better sleep quality, reduced anxiety and depression risk, decreased pain sensitivity, and more.

Mindfulness creates stillness and space within us. We learn how to respond versus react. By learning to be in the moment, we're also offered the opportunity to embrace and savor what is happening. That stillness and space offers us new possibilities of expanding and growing the goodness that is already present in our lives, no matter how seemingly small or large.

Promoting Gratitude and Joy with Mindfulness

Mindfulness is the practice of being fully connected with your thoughts and feelings without getting caught up in them. It helps us quickly identify our triggers—situations that cause stress—and break the cycle by responding differently and more positively. Breathwork is also a positive action that can help you cope with overwhelm because it creates space between you and your thoughts and emotions so that you don't get caught up in them as much. For example, if your mind often says, "I'm so overwhelmed," try connecting with yourself through breathwork.

Take a deep breath into your belly. Close your eyes. Place one hand on your heart and one on your lower belly / hip. Take three long breaths through your nose, then exhale through pursed lips (like a walrus). Inhale deeply again two more times, then exhale slowly.

This will not only calm down the stress hormones in the body but also increase blood flow to the brain, leading to clarity and focus.

The Benefits of Gratitude

There are a lot of reasons why gratitude is considered to be so important. Gratitude increases happiness and positive emotions, decreases stress levels, and improves sleep. It also reduces depression and anxiety, both of which are linked to several health issues.

One of the most significant benefits of gratitude is that it allows you to make meaning out of any situation. If you think your life sucks, look at all the good things in it, which may be more than you initially thought. Acknowledging what makes your life worth living will help alleviate stress and anxiety, making gratitude a powerful tool for mental health improvement.

The Benefits of Joy

There are many physical benefits of joy. One of the most apparent benefits is that happy thoughts and feelings can improve your mood and decrease stress levels. In this way, joy can help you sleep better, which has long-term health benefits for your body and mind. Happiness also increases blood flow to the brain, which improves concentration.

Joy can help you make better decisions. Those who experience positive emotions such as joy and amusement are more likely to exercise self-control and make wise choices because they are less likely to focus on regrets or negative emotions when making decisions. Feeling joy can help motivate us to take action and care for ourselves physically and mentally. It also gives us a greater sense of fulfillment and satisfaction.

The emotional benefits of joy are obvious but worth noting. Joy releases endorphins that make us feel good, like an instant natural high. When we feel good, we naturally want to share those emotions with others: We smile more and laugh more.

Emotions are contagious and can spread between people in bad and good ways. When someone is feeling joy, it affects the people around them. This spreading is important: it helps people feel connected to each other, creates a positive atmosphere, and improves relationships and emotional connections.

The spiritual benefit of joy is that it frees us from the labels of what we are and gives us a chance to not worry about what may come. It is a state of being in which we stop feeling like we need to be anything other than who we are. Joy helps us accomplish our goals more easily because it energizes and inspires us. As a result, joy also increases productivity and engagement in your day-to-day activities. When you are joyful, you tend to be less reactive (e.g., you don't get frustrated when things don't go your way). And when you're less reactive, you can respond with kindness rather than anger or frustration. In addition, joy can help you remain positive in the face of difficult situations and problems by reminding you that there is value in each moment, even if it seems daunting at first glance. Joy can also help you stay motivated as it motivates others around you. Being surrounded by joyful people helps build self-confidence, which can increase happiness levels for everyone involved (i.e., family members, friends, colleagues.)

Joy Increases Your Quality of Life

Coined by Dr. Barbara Fredrickson, the broaden-and-build theory is about how positive emotions can help people grow and develop. Just like how negative emotions can make us feel small, positive emotions can make us feel bigger and better. When we feel good, we are more likely to try new things, meet new people, and learn new things. The theory goes that the more positive emotions we feel, the more we will grow and develop as people. Essentially, joy not only begets more joy but also creates more positive emotions that drastically improve our quality of life.

Regarding the benefits, joy and gratitude are not the only antidotes to stress and overwhelm. They can also produce an overflow of positive emotions and an improved quality of life.

Meditation

People spend hours every day engaged in activities that don't require much thought or concentration, such as driving to work, checking social media, and listening to music. When we allow our minds to wander, we daydream or think about irrelevant things. While these moments can be enjoyable, focusing on the present moment is crucial so as not to let our minds wander. Mindfulness meditation involves focusing on your breathing and relaxing your mind through techniques such as paying attention to your body or repeating a phrase silently to yourself. Therefore, mindfulness meditation can help you become more aware of your surroundings and slow down your brain so that you are less susceptible to unhelpful thoughts creeping into your mind.

Meditation in Motion

Yoga is about finding balance within your body and mind. In this practice, you spend time moving in a mindful way to help your body and mind connect. It's often referred to as the "meditation in motion," meaning that while you're experiencing the physical sensations of movement, your mind will also be able to find peace.

One step for bringing more joy and gratitude into your life is to practice yoga regularly. Practicing asanas (physical postures) daily can help increase your physical health, improve your balance and flexibility, strengthen your muscles, clear your mind, and make you feel more centered. Yoga also offers various levels, from beginner to advanced-level practices, allowing you to find something that works for you and your body.

The benefits of yoga don't stop when you leave the studio. Yoga helps people see themselves in a different light and start to feel good about themselves. When your body is strong and healthy, it makes you feel good about yourself because it reflects who you are inside. And when you know yourself more deeply, it starts feeling like there's so much more joy in life than before.

Yoga is one of the most potent ways to bring more gratitude into your life. In many ways, yoga is a practice that requires you to challenge your perspective. On the mat, you'll encounter poses that would be challenging for most people, but with practice and patience, you could master them and begin to see benefits in your life. Once you succeed with a pose or type of yoga, move on to something more challenging. When you challenge yourself, you'll take your perspective to the next level and help you increase your gratitude. We recommend starting with basic poses that are easy for beginners to try, such as downward-facing dog and savasana (corpse pose). If you practice yoga, these are some of the poses associated with increased happiness: virasana (hero pose), low seated forward fold, anjanasana (anger pose), sukhasana (easy pose), parivritta trikonasana (revolved triangle pose), utkatasana (chair pose), ardha chandrasana (half-moon pose), upavistha konasana (wide-angle seated forward bend), parsvottanasna (intense side stretch), and urdhva dhanurasana or upavishtha dhanurasana (crow posture / wheel posture).

Breathwork

An often overlooked aspect of yoga is the breath. *Pranayama* is a word that means "yoga of life or breath." It's often referred to as the practice of regulating one's breathing, which can be done by practicing various breathing exercises.

One exercise you can do to help you breathe more deeply is called alternate nostril breathing. This exercise can be done in any position, and it opens your nasal passages and calms your mind. Alternate nostril breathing can also reduce stress and increase feelings of peace and happiness.

Another essential aspect of pranayama is deep concentration. This exercise aims to focus on one thing for a certain amount of time, usually about fifteen minutes or more. During this time, your attention should be solely focused on what you are concentrating on; try not to think about anything else during that time.

Pranayama has several other benefits, including improved mental health and increased brain function, reduced hypertension risk, reduced anxiety, improved sleep quality, better digestion and immunity function, an overall reduction in stress levels, and greater mindfulness (and consequently a happier state).

How to Bring Mindfulness into Your Yoga Practice

Mindfulness helps us look at situations from a more balanced perspective—and it's an essential tool for dealing with overwhelm when it arises. It's easy to integrate mindfulness into your yoga practice. One way is to simply bring awareness into your poses by focusing on sensations as they happen instead of thinking about what they should be like. For example, when you're moving into downward dog, focus how your hips feel and if there's any tension in those muscles before you move into the pose rather than perfect alignment. Another way is to have short, guided meditation sessions before or after your practice in which you set aside time to be mindful of yourself and what's happening inside your body.

While practicing mindfulness may seem daunting at first, it's as easy as bringing this mindful awareness into every aspect of your life—whether it be through yoga or other activities like cooking or spending time with loved ones.

How to Be More Mindful in Everyday Life

If you want to learn to be more mindful in everyday life, the first step is to let go of any expectations you have for yourself. Letting yourself off the hook can be challenging when you constantly try to reach a particular goal or experience. Whether your goal is getting a promotion, losing weight, or finding love—if you continuously strive to meet these goals and don't let yourself off the hook when you aren't satisfied, there will come the point where you will give up. It will help if you have time and space to process what has happened and come back stronger than ever. Accept that you can't change everything about the world or control everything that happens to you. You cannot win every battle, so nothing will ever get done if you focus on fighting every battle.

Next, relax and accept that there will be times when things don't go your way. The key is being able to handle those moments without being overwhelmed. Once you have achieved acceptance, it will become easier for you to slow down and take a deep breath during those difficult moments.

Be Aware of Your Thoughts

Focus on what you're doing now rather than worrying about the past or future. When you practice mindfulness, you see situations from a different perspective, which can help you solve problems that may have been impossible to solve before.

The more you are mindful, the better your ability to pay attention will be. When you feel like you need to constantly be doing something or there's a voice in the back of your head telling you that you're not good enough or that everything is going to go wrong, it might be time to stop. This doesn't mean giving up on your goals and ambitions but instead finding a way to care for yourself without being so hard on yourself. You can start by paying attention to what is going on in your mind. Notice the thoughts coming into your head and how they make you feel. If something is bothering you, pay attention to the feeling in your body at those times too. Paying attention might help relieve some tension when you are stuck in unfavorable self-talk and toxic thoughts without acknowledging them or changing your perspective. Know what triggers negative thoughts and learn to avoid them before they start.

Mindful Breathing

Mindful breathing is an integral part of mindfulness practice. Conscious breathing simply means paying attention to your breath. When we are mindful of our breath, we are better able to be present at the moment and aware of our thoughts and emotions. Breathing mindfully can help us to reduce stress, anxiety, and depression. It can also allow us to focus our attention and improve our concentration. How is mindful breathing done?

Simply focus your attention on the physical sensations of each breath. Count each breath from when you breathe in to when you breathe out. When thoughts arise, let them go and return to counting. Each time you remember to do this that is one breath. Feel your body as you breathe in and out, focusing on the physical sensation of breathing in and out. Notice how it feels to breathe in and then to breathe out.

Gratitude Journaling

In recent years, gratitude journaling has become popular as a way to boost overall happiness and well-being. The benefits of gratitude journaling are backed up by science. Research from the *Journal of Happiness Studies* suggests that writing down what you're grateful for can increase happiness, improve your health, and help you sleep better.[1]

The concept is simple: each day, take some time to write down a few things you're grateful for. This could be anything from big blessings like good health or a new job to smaller things such as a sunny day or a delicious meal. You could also take a few minutes to list your blessings if you're feeling stressed or anxious or have had a rough day. You don't have to be spiritual or religious to practice gratitude journaling. The most important part of your journaling practice is staying consistent.

Sound Meditation

Sound meditation is a powerful tool that can help to improve your mental and physical well-being. By using sound to focus your attention, you can achieve a deeper level of relaxation, happiness, and peace. The type of music or sound that you use for your meditation will depend on what you want to accomplish. For example, some sound meditations use only one type of sound, such as a gong or singing bowl. Other sound meditations may use a variety of sounds, such as nature sounds or music.

Sit comfortably in a quiet place where you can relax and listen to the sound without being disturbed. Listen to the sound with

---

1. Steven M. Toepfer, Kelly Cichy, and Patti Peters, "Letters of Gratitude: Further Evidence for Author Benefits," *Journal of Happiness Studies* 13, no. 1 (April 2012): 187–201, https://doi.org/10.1007/s10902-011-9257-7.

your eyes closed and focus on the inner experience of listening. Allow yourself to enter into a deep state of relaxation and calmness. After a few minutes, when your mind is relaxed and focused, let the sound fade into silence. When ready to return to daily activity, slowly open your eyes and stretch. Take some time to reflect on your experience of this particular type of meditation.

The Impact of Technology on Mindfulness

The digital age has brought with it many technological innovations that have helped make our world more convenient but at the cost of some lifestyle changes that have affected our mental health. We are constantly surrounded by screens and gadgets that allow us to stay connected to the world at large. The constant presence of screens has also created a severe problem: overstimulation. As we become more immersed in digital life, we forget how to be present. How often does technology allow us to engage fully during a mindful moment? For the most part, technology has replaced mindfulness, which is why becoming aware again can only happen by disconnecting from technology. To combat these effects, we see an increasing number of people choosing to disconnect from the digital world and explore other ways of engaging with it instead.

As tech-free mindful moments become more prevalent, people can refresh themselves while still being connected to the world to help them maintain their sanity as they reconnect with friends and family without getting overwhelmed with their digital life.

As the digital world continues to evolve rapidly, new methods of connecting with technology will continue to be introduced. Digital technologies have the potential to help us develop our mindfulness skills and engage in a more mindful way with technology, a fact that will likely become even more prevalent as the digital age advances. It's therefore important for us all to learn to engage with technology more intentionally to live more conscious lives.

There are a variety of apps and tools that can help you engage more consciously with technology. Some apps, such as Headspace, have been designed to help people practice mindfulness using their phones or computer. This app uses guided meditations, both audio and video, to help individuals focus on what is happening in the present moment rather than what is happening in their heads.

As technology continues to transform the way we live both digitally and physically, how can we ensure that we stay mindful? Here are four tips for balancing your mindfulness practices with technology. Stop checking social media all day. Know where your information is coming from and trust its source. Take care of yourself mentally and physically by practicing mindfulness exercises throughout the day. Remember that technology can bring you closer to others just as much as it can isolate you from others, so don't neglect your interpersonal relationships when online.

Technology has made us more connected and has provided us with many life-changing innovations. However, it is essential to remember that it takes a balance between technology and mindfulness. It is important to focus on those moments where technology is not necessary and to find ways to use it mindfully. When mindful, we can be present in the moment. By being aware of the present moment, we can focus on what is happening around us instead of being distracted by the world around us.

CONTRIBUTOR
BIOGRAPHIES

Gail Bussi is a writer, artist, kitchen witch, and professional cook. After running a catering company and writing a cookbook, she returned to her long-held interest in herbs and green magic. Gail has studied holistic herbalism, natural healing, and mindfulness. She is the author of *Enchanted Herbal*, *Enchanted Kitchen*, and *Enchanted Teatime*.

Jiulio Consiglio is a spiritual teacher and author who focuses on the transformative power of inner stillness, the mind-body-spirit connection and psychic abilities development. His message is that there is life beyond fear and incessant thinking and it is found in the dimension of inner stillness. Jiulio currently offers his consciousness-based teachings to individuals and groups. He is the author of *Open Your Third Eye*.

Cyndi Dale is an internationally renowned author, speaker, healer, and business consultant. She is president of Life Systems Services, through which she has assisted more than 70,000 clients and students and presented training classes throughout Europe, Asia, and the Americas. Cyndi is the author of nearly thirty books, including *Llewellyn's Complete Book of Chakras*, *The Spiritual Power of Empathy*, and *Energy Healing for Trauma, Stress & Chronic Illness*. She lives in Minneapolis, Minnesota. Visit her at www.CyndiDale.com.

Emily A. Francis has a BS in Exercise Science and Wellness and a Master's Degree in Human Performance. She is the author of *Stretch Therapy*, *The Body Heals Itself*, *Whole Body Healing*, *Healing Ourselves Whole*, and *The Taste of Joy*. You can find her at www.EmilyAFrancisBooks.com.

Melanie C. Klein, MA, is an empowerment coach, thought leader, and influencer in the areas of body confidence, authentic empowerment, and visibility. She is also a successful writer, speaker, and professor of sociology and women's studies. She co-founded the Yoga and Body Image Coalition in 2014. She is the coeditor of *Yoga and Body Image*; *Yoga, the Body and Embodied Social Change*, *Yoga Rising*, and *Embodied Resilience through Yoga*. She's also a contributor in *21st Century Yoga* and featured in *Conversations with Modern Yogis* and *Llewellyn's Complete Book of Mindful Living*.

Marc Cordon is the founder of Greater Good Strategic & Life Coaching which serves rebellious entrepreneurs, misfit coaches, and ostensible iconoclasts who are committed to changing history for the better. For over two decades, he has assisted countless people in self-development through speaking engagements, retreats, mini-courses, and one-on-one advising and mentoring. Marc splits his time between Tampa, Florida, and Atlanta, Georgia, where he loves spending time with his family and playing roller derby under the nickname of Manila Ice.

Chanda Parkinson is a psychic intuitive and spiritual mentor who utilizes her spiritual gifts, tarot, and astrology to support others through transitions in life with clarity and deep compassion. Creator of the Soul Path Consulting Program, she brings her clients to a place of deep understanding of the intricate nuances of their own soul's path. She is the author of *Meditations for Psychic Development*. Visit her online at www. chandaparkinson.com.

Leah Patterson is a grounded, ultra-creative woman with deep spiritual roots. Whether through dance, herbal healing, spiritual divination, or any of the other ways she works, her mission in life has always been to help people live a more on-purpose, holistically fulfilling, and audaciously happy life. She's studied astrology, the tarot, herbal medicine, aromatherapy and other healing modalities for more than twenty years and uses these in her toolbox to help her clients transform.

Kristy Robinett is a revolutionary psychic medium and astrologer. In addition to giving readings and teaching workshops, she uses her psychic skills to assist with police investigations. Kristy lectures across the country and is a frequent media commentator, appearing on the ID Channel's *Restless Souls, Fox News, ABC News, Coast to Coast,* and more. She is the author of several books, including *Born Under a Good Sign, It's a Wonderful Afterlife,* and *Embrace Your Empathy.* Visit her online at http://www.KristyRobinett.com.

Amy B. Scher is a leading voice in the field of mind-body-spirit healing. As an energy therapist, Amy uses energy therapy techniques to help those experiencing illness and those in need of emotional healing. She has been featured on healthcare blogs, CNN, *Curve* magazine, *Elephant Journal,* and the *San Francisco Book Review.* She is the author of many books, including *How to Heal Yourself When No One Else Can* and *How to Heal Yourself from Anxiety When No One Else Can.* Amy was also named one of *Advocate*'s "40 Under 40" for 2013. Visit her online at www.amybscher.com.

Shai Tubali is an international speaker, author, and spiritual teacher. He is one of Europe's leading authorities in the field of chakras and the subtle body and has published twelve books including *Seven Day Chakras* and *Llewellyn's Complete Guide to Meditation.* Shai founded Human Greatness, an international center in Berlin. Visit him online at www.shaitubali.com.

Angela A. Wix is an acquiring and developmental editor for books on personal transformation, wellness, and spirituality. She is also an artist, poet, and author of five books (two published and three in-process): *Llewellyn's Little Book of Unicorns*, *The Secret Psychic*, *Your Pain Is Real*, *I Am Strong (and other things i tell myself)*, and *One Beautiful Thing*. Visit her at AngelaAnn.Wix.com/arts and @AngelaAWix on Facebook and Instagram.

Shannon Yrizarry is a certified yoga teacher and professional clairvoyant who has written extensively in the wellness field. She teaches meditation and leads workshops on transforming the physical and emotional self through living a yogic lifestyle. She is also a certified Reiki practitioner and has done astrology readings, dream interpretations, and tarot for celebrities and television. Shannon is the author of *Psychic Yoga*, *Kundalini Energy*, and *Connect and Work with Spirit Guides*.

To Write to the Editor

If you wish to contact the authors or Editor or would like more information about this book, please write to the author in care of Llewellyn Worldwide Ltd. and we will forward your request. Both the author and publisher appreciate hearing from you and learning of your enjoyment of this book and how it has helped you. Llewellyn Worldwide Ltd. cannot guarantee that every letter written to the author can be answered, but all will be forwarded. Please write to:

Angela A. Wix
⅏ Llewellyn Worldwide
2143 Wooddale Drive
Woodbury, MN 55125-2989

Please enclose a self-addressed stamped envelope for reply,
or $1.00 to cover costs. If outside the U.S.A., enclose
an international postal reply coupon.

Many of Llewellyn's authors have websites with additional information and resources. For more information, please visit our website at http://www.llewellyn.com